Roger Quilter
55 Songs

Low Voice

Edited by Richard Walters

This publication is not for sale in the
EU or other European countries.

ISBN 978-0-634-06009-0

7777 W. BLUEMOUND RD. P.O. BOX 13819 MILWAUKEE, WI 53213

Copyright © 2003 by HAL LEONARD CORPORATION
International Copyright Secured. All Rights Reserved.

For all works contained herein:
Unauthorized copying, arranging, adapting, recording or public performance is an infringement of copyright.
Infringers are liable under the law.

Visit Hal Leonard Online at
www.halleonard.com

Contents
by Opus Number

Three Songs of the Sea, Op. 1
- 7   The Sea-Bird
- 10   Moonlight
- 13   By the Sea

Two Songs (1903)
- 16   Come Back!
- 18   A Secret

from Three Songs, Op. 3
- 20   Love's Philosophy
- 25   Now sleeps the crimson petal

- 28   June (1905)

from Four Child Songs, Op. 5
- 32   A Good Child
- 36   The Lamplighter
- 41   Where Go the Boats?

Three Shakespeare Songs, Op. 6 (First Set)
- 44   Come away, death
- 49   O mistress mine
- 52   Blow, blow, thou winter wind

To Julia, Op. 8
- 59   Prelude
- 60   The Bracelet
- 64   The Maiden Blush
- 66   To Daisies
- 69   The Night Piece
- 76   Julia's Hair
- 78   Interlude
- 79   Cherry Ripe

Seven Elizabethan Lyrics, Op. 12
- 90   Weep you no more
- 94   My Life's Delight
- 98   Damask Roses
- 85   The Faithless Shepherdess
- 100   Brown is my love
- 102   By a Fountainside
- 106   Fair House of Joy

Because "Prelude" and "Interlude" from *To Julia* are piano only, they are not tallied in the "55 Songs" of the title of this volume.

Four Songs, Op. 14
- 110 Autumn Evening
- 114 April
- 117 A Last Year's Rose
- 121 Song of the Blackbird

Six Songs, Op. 18
Three Songs for Baritone or Tenor:
- 125 To Wine and Beauty
- 129 Where be you going?
- 133 The Jocund Dance

- 138 The Spring is at the door

Two September Songs:
- 142 Through the sunny garden
- 145 The Valley and the Hill

Three Songs of William Blake, Op. 20
- 148 Dream Valley
- 150 The Wild Flower's Song
- 153 Daybreak

Three Pastoral Songs, Op. 22
- 156 I will go with my father a-ploughing
- 161 Cherry Valley
- 164 I wish and I wish

Five Shakespeare Songs, Op. 23 (Second Set)
- 172 Fear no more the heat o' the sun
- 169 Under the greenwood tree
- 176 It was a lover and his lass
- 182 Take, O take those lips away
- 184 Hey, ho, the wind and the rain

Two Songs, Op. 26
- 188 In the highlands
- 193 Over the land is April

Old English Popular Songs (later incorporated into The Arnold Book of Old Songs)
- 199 Barbara Allen
- 204 Drink to Me Only with Thine Eyes
- 207 The Jolly Miller
- 212 Over the Mountains
- 218 Three Poor Mariners

- 222 Notes on the Songs

Contents
Alphabetically by Song Title

114	April	28	June
110	Autumn Evening	36	The Lamplighter
199	Barbara Allen	117	A Last Year's Rose
52	Blow, blow, thou winter wind	20	Love's Philosophy
60	The Bracelet	64	The Maiden Blush
100	Brown is my love	10	Moonlight
102	By a Fountainside	94	My Life's Delight
13	By the Sea	69	The Night Piece
79	Cherry Ripe	25	Now sleeps the crimson petal
161	Cherry Valley	49	O mistress mine
44	Come away, death	193	Over the land is April
16	Come Back!	212	Over the Mountains
98	Damask Roses	59	Prelude
153	Daybreak	7	The Sea-Bird
148	Dream Valley	18	A Secret
204	Drink to Me Only with Thine Eyes	121	Song of the Blackbird
106	Fair House of Joy	138	The Spring is at the door
85	The Faithless Shepherdess	182	Take, o take those lips away
172	Fear no more the heat o' the sun	218	Three Poor Mariners
32	A Good Child	142	Through the sunny garden
184	Hey, ho, the wind and the rain	66	To Daisies
156	I will go with my father a-ploughing	125	To Wine and Beauty
164	I wish and I wish	169	Under the greenwood tree
188	In the highlands	145	The Valley and the Hill
78	Interlude	90	Weep you no more
176	It was a lover and his lass	129	Where be you going?
133	The Jocund Dance	41	Where Go the Boats?
207	The Jolly Miller	150	The Wild Flower's Song
76	Julia's Hair		

Poet Index

Anonymous
- 199 Barbara Allen
- 207 The Jolly Miller
- 218 Three Poor Mariners

Anonymous Elizabethan
- 100 Brown is my love
- 98 Damask Roses
- 106 Fair House of Joy
- 85 The Faithless Shepherdess
- 90 Weep you no more

William Blake
- 153 Daybreak
- 148 Dream Valley
- 133 The Jocund Dance
- 150 The Wild Flower's Song

Joseph Campbell
- 161 Cherry Valley
- 156 I will go with my father a-ploughing
- 164 I wish and I wish

Thomas Campion
- 94 My Life's Delight

Mary Coleridge
- 142 Through the sunny garden
- 145 The Valley and the Hill

Earl of Rochester
- 125 To Wine and Beauty

W.E. Henley
- 117 A Last Year's Rose
- 121 Song of the Blackbird

Robert Herrick
- 60 The Bracelet
- 79 Cherry Ripe
- 76 Julia's Hair
- 64 The Maiden Blush
- 69 The Night Piece
- 66 To Daisies

Nora Hopper
- 28 June
- 138 The Spring is at the door

Ben Jonson
- 102 By a Fountainside
- 204 Drink to Me Only with Thine Eyes

John Keats
- 129 Where be you going?

Arthur Marquarie
- 110 Autumn Evening

Thomas Percy
- 212 Over the Mountains

Roger Quilter
- 13 By the Sea
- 16 Come Back!
- 10 Moonlight
- 7 The Sea-Bird
- 18 A Secret

William Shakespeare
- 44 Come away, death
- 52 Blow, blow, thou winter wind
- 172 Fear no more the heat o' the sun
- 184 Hey, ho, the wind and the rain
- 176 It was a lover and his lass
- 49 O mistress mine
- 182 Take, O take those lips away
- 169 Under the greenwood tree

Percy B. Shelley
- 20 Love's Philosophy

Robert Louis Stevenson
- 32 A Good Child
- 188 In the highlands
- 36 The Lamplighter
- 193 Over the land is April
- 41 Where Go the Boats?

Alfred Tennyson
- 25 Now sleeps the crimson petal

William Watson
- 114 April

Roger Quilter (born 1 November 1877, died 21 September 1953) was a breed of composer that has rarely existed after the first decades of the twentieth century: he was overwhelmingly concerned with the art song. His preoccupation with the genre spanned more than fifty years, from his youth until near his death, more than fifty years later, resulting in roughly 140 songs in total.

Quilter was born into a wealthy family in Sussex, England. His father, William Cuthbert Quilter, was a prominent, very successful businessman, art collector and member of Parliament, and was knighted Sir Quilter by Queen Victoria in 1897. There were seven children in the Quilter home who survived past infancy, two girls and five boys. Roger was fifth oldest. This tall, lanky, sensitive, artistic boy was miserable in the traditional, sports-minded population of males at Eton College. He went abroad to study composition with Ivann Knorr in Frankfurt at the Hoch Conservatory. Fellow students there, at different times, included Percy Grainger, Balfour Gardiner, Norman O'Neill and Cyril Scott. Grainger, particularly, became a lifelong close friend of Quilter's.

A public career began for Quilter with the 1901 London premiere of *Songs of the Sea*, not surprisingly the composer's choice for the designation of Opus 1. Gervase Elwes, a celebrated tenor, became interested in Quilter songs. For him the composer wrote the song cycle *To Julia*, which Elwes premiered in 1905. The same singer gave the first performance of the *Seven Elizabethan Lyrics* in 1908. Quilter's music soon gained favor, and his songs were regularly performed, particularly in London. A good pianist, the composer often served as accompanist in recital. Quilter's wide social circles included just about any musician of note who worked in London in the first decades of the twentieth century.

Due to inheritance, Quilter never had to seek employment, leaving his time and mind free for composing, though his life was not always a happy one. His wealth was limited, and in later years he was often in debt. He was plagued by chronic poor health throughout his life, which prevented military service during World War I. Quilter was a well-mannered, sophisticated gentleman, with the polish of his well-to-do social class, but with a constantly observable nervousness. He suffered unstable periods, with pronounced mental illness in the years leading to his death. A homosexual, he never married, though he formed a few close attachments and had devoted friends and supporters.

The composer's chamber instrumental and orchestral output was limited; most was light in nature. Most were arrangements of music composed for other genres. Quilter also composed piano pieces, small choral works, two ballets, and incidental theatre music, notably for *Where the Rainbow Ends*, a children's fairy play with music first produced in 1911, with annual Christmastime revivals in London until 1959. (Noel Coward was in the original cast.) The composer collaborated on the light opera *Julia*, which premiered in 1936 at the Royal Opera House in London, but to not much success.

Quilter valued graceful elegance and a love of words, both qualities that are evident in his songs and his idiomatic phrasing for the voice. The imagery in his songs constantly reflects his boyhood countryside of southern England. He was uninterested in the more extreme and progressive artistic trends of the twentieth century. In general, though there are exceptions, he showed a rather refined literary taste in poetry chosen for his songs, with an inherent nationalist British identification. Quilter's fluid and distinctive musical style, though occasionally dramatic, is most often infused with a natural, creamy English charm, though he did not compose quickly, and labored over every detail. Most agree that his best work was created rather young in his life, before his mid-forties.

Today Quilter would be considered a minor historical figure in British music overall. Regarding art song, however, very few composers working in English have matched his achievement of a living body of beloved, relevant, literate repertoire.

RW

To my mother

THE SEA-BIRD

from Three Songs of the Sea, Op. 1

original key

Words and Music by
Roger Quilter
Op. 1, No. 1

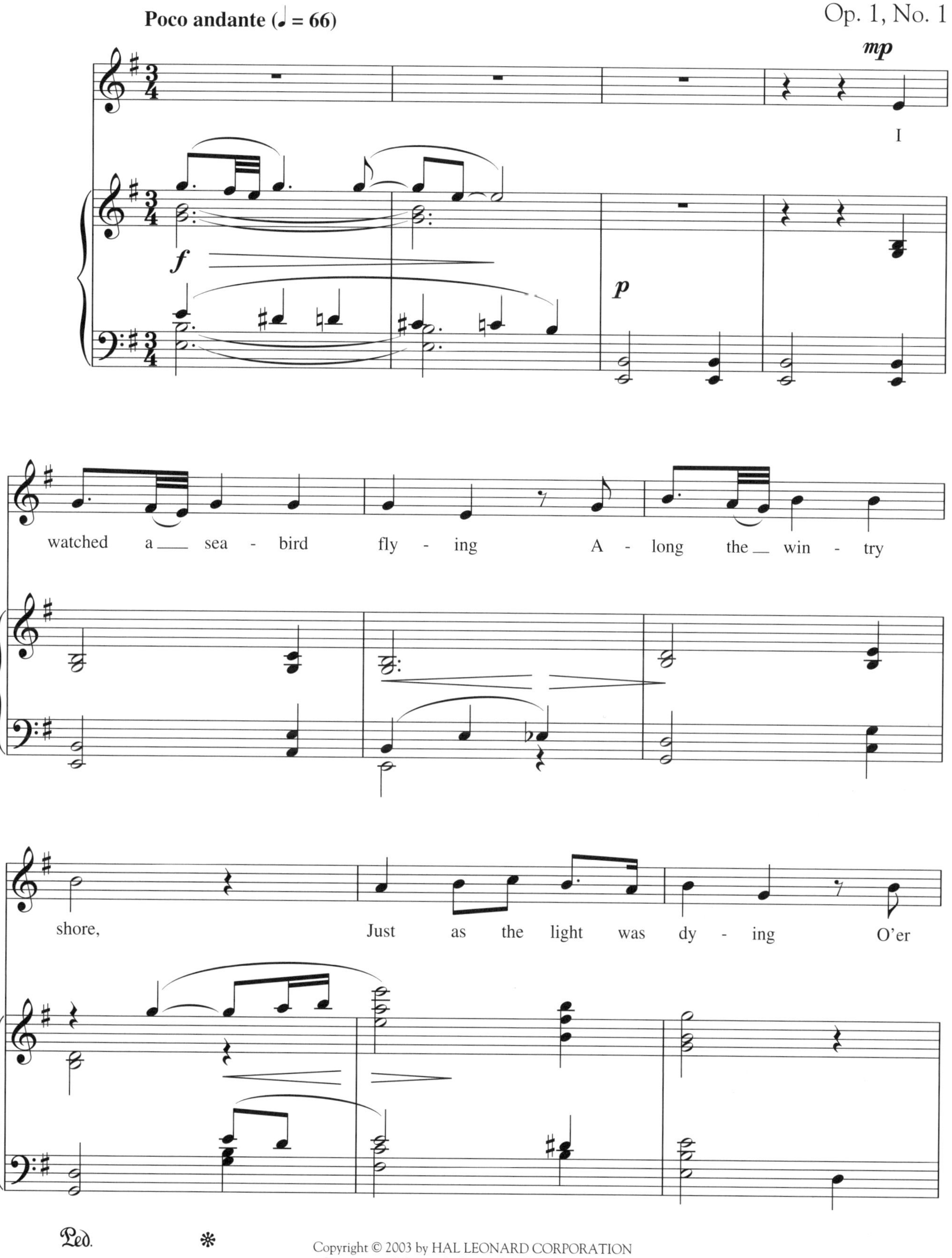

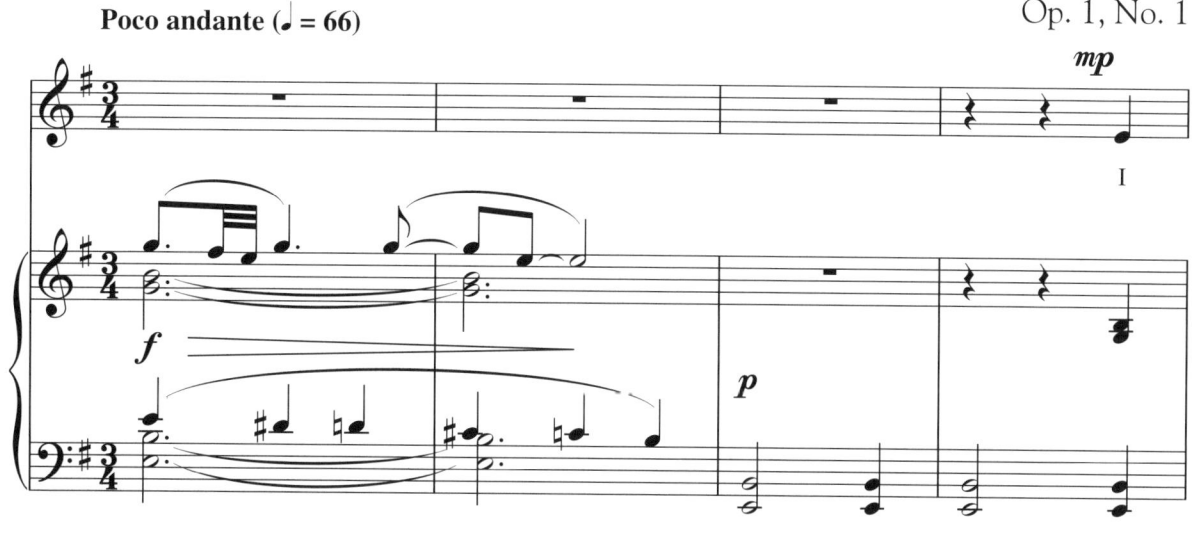

To my mother

MOONLIGHT
from Three Songs of the Sea, Op. 1
original key

Words and Music by
Roger Quilter
Op. 1, No. 2

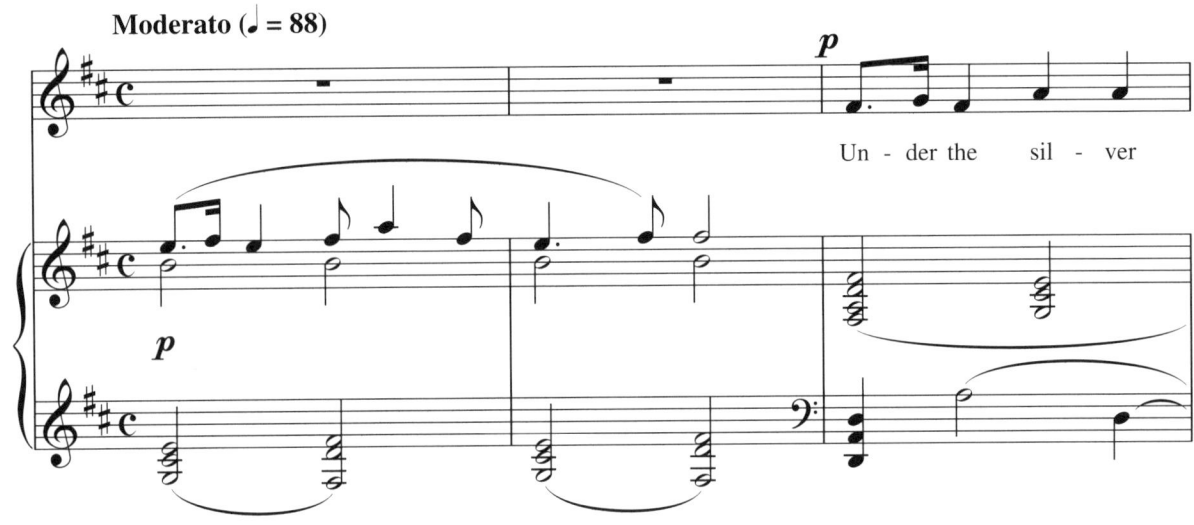

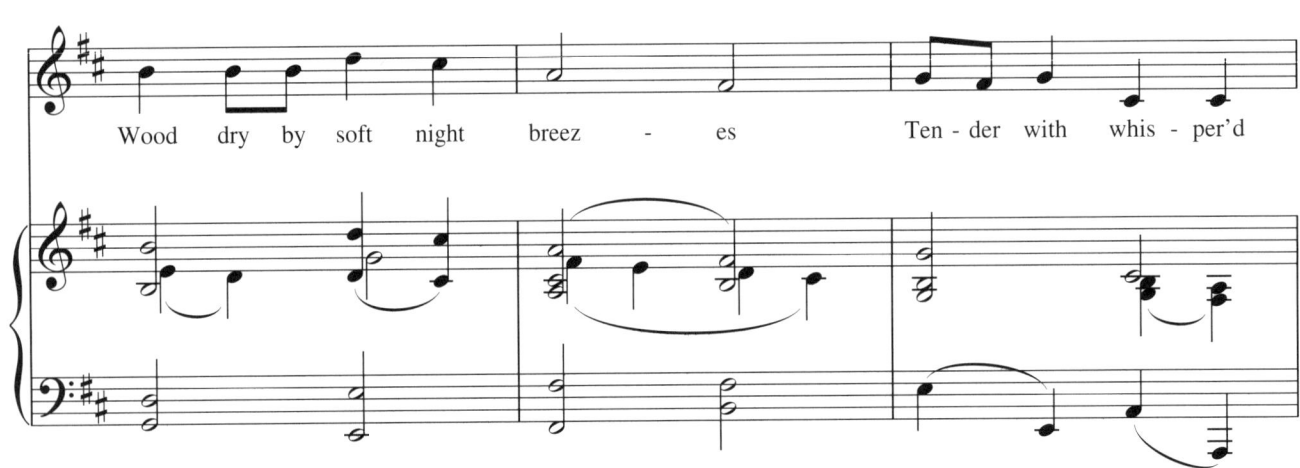

Copyright © 2003 by HAL LEONARD CORPORATION
International Copyright Secured   All Rights Reserved

To my mother
BY THE SEA
from Three Songs of the Sea, Op. 1
original key

Words and Music by
Roger Quilter
Op. 1, No. 3

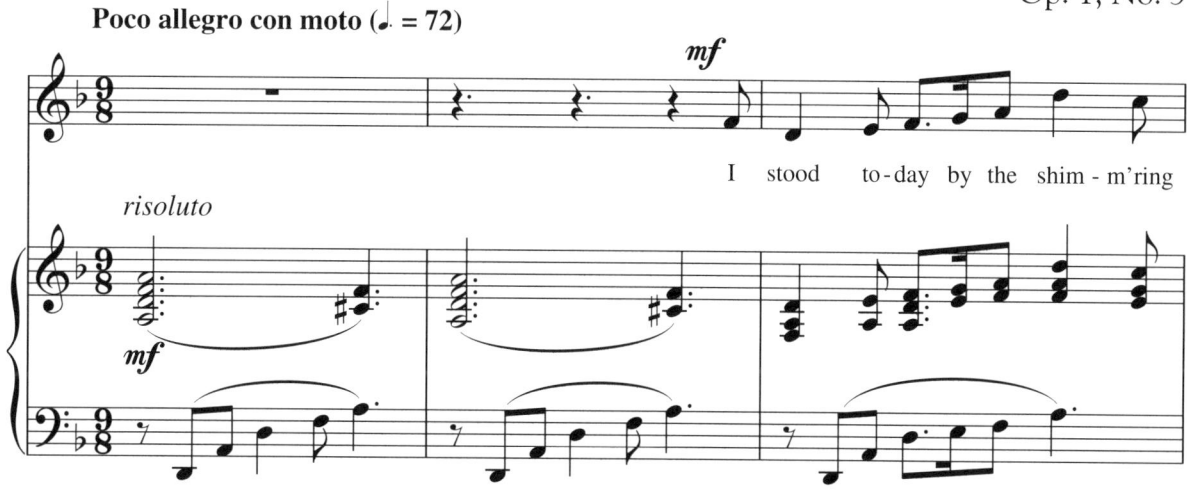

Copyright © 2003 by HAL LEONARD CORPORATION
International Copyright Secured   All Rights Reserved

COME BACK!
from Two Songs (1903)
original key: C minor

Words and Music by
Roger Quilter

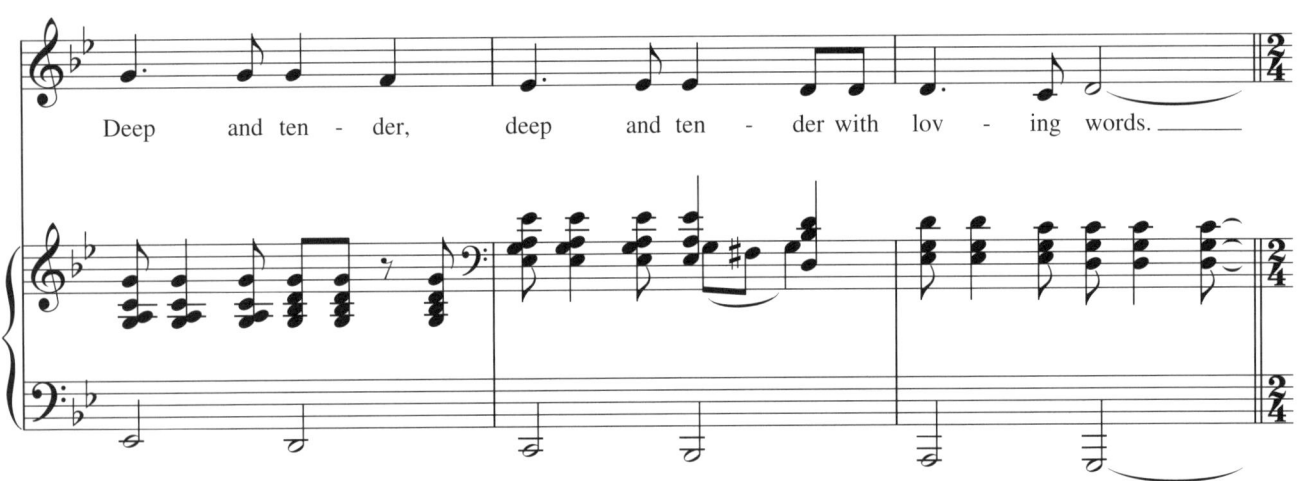

Copyright © 2003 by HAL LEONARD CORPORATION
International Copyright Secured   All Rights Reserved

A SECRET
from Two Songs (1903)
original key: E-flat Major

Words and Music by
Roger Quilter

Copyright © 2003 by HAL LEONARD CORPORATION
International Copyright Secured   All Rights Reserved

LOVE'S PHILOSOPHY
To Gervase Elwes
from Three Songs, Op. 3
original key: F Major

Words by
Percy B. Shelley

Music by
Roger Quilter
Op. 3, No. 1

NOW SLEEPS THE CRIMSON PETAL
from Three Songs, Op. 3
original key: E-flat Major

To Mrs. E.P. Balmain

Words by
Alfred Tennyson

Music by
Roger Quilter
Op. 3, No. 2

Now sleeps the crim-son pe-tal, not the white;

Nor waves the cy-press in the pa-lace walk;

Copyright © 2003 by HAL LEONARD CORPORATION
International Copyright Secured All Rights Reserved

Words by
Nora Hopper

To Miss Ada Crossley
JUNE
original key: D Major

Music by
Roger Quilter
1905

Copyright © 2003 by HAL LEONARD CORPORATION
International Copyright Secured   All Rights Reserved

32

To my sister, Norah

A GOOD CHILD
from Four Child Songs, Op. 5
original key: F Major

Words by
Robert Louis Stevenson

Music by
Roger Quilter
Op. 5, No. 1

Copyright © 2003 by HAL LEONARD CORPORATION
International Copyright Secured   All Rights Reserved

To my sister, Norah

THE LAMPLIGHTER
from Four Child Songs, Op. 5
original key: E-flat Major

Words by
Robert Louis Stevenson

Music by
Roger Quilter
Op. 5, No. 2

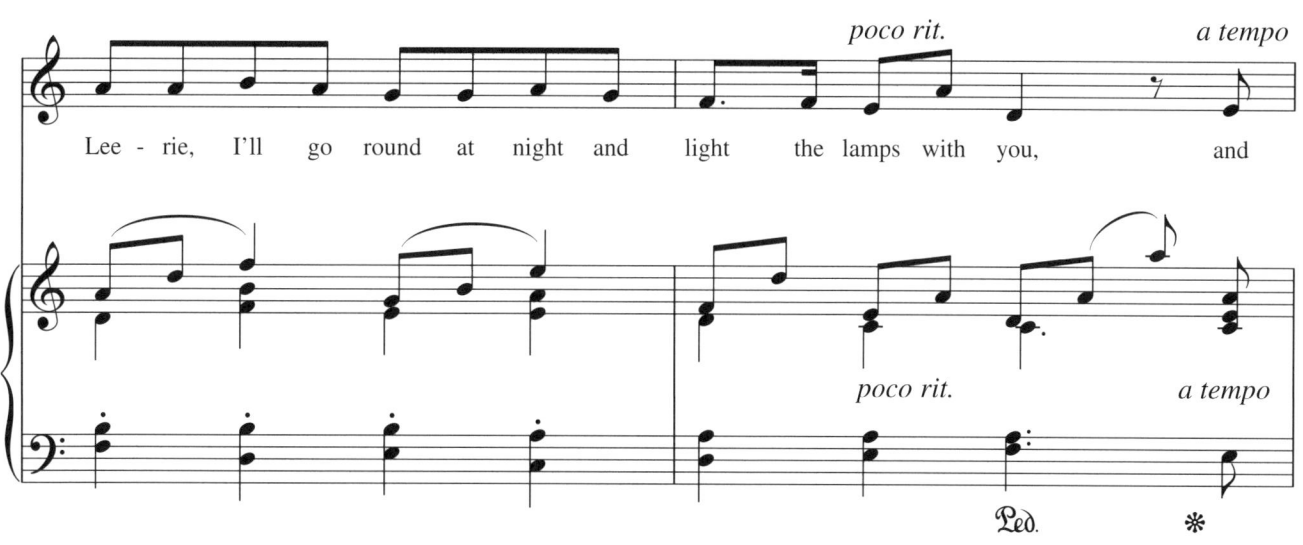
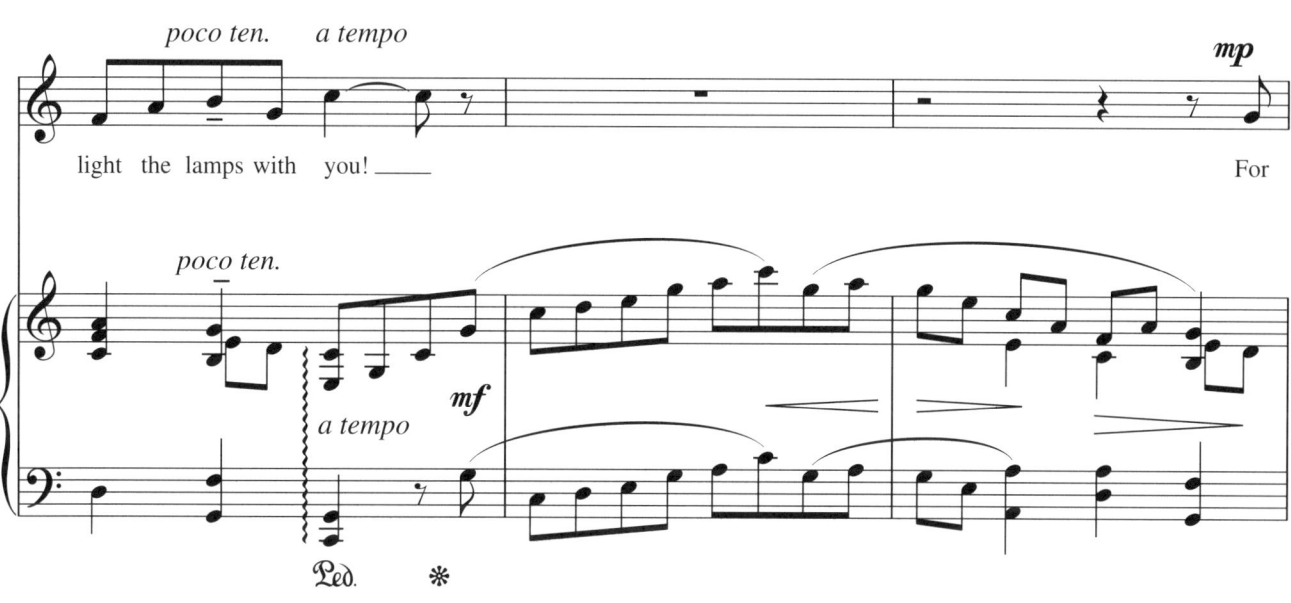

To my sister, Norah

WHERE GO THE BOATS?

from Four Child Songs, op. 5
original key: A Major

Words by
Robert Louis Stevenson

Music by
Roger Quilter
Op. 5, No. 3

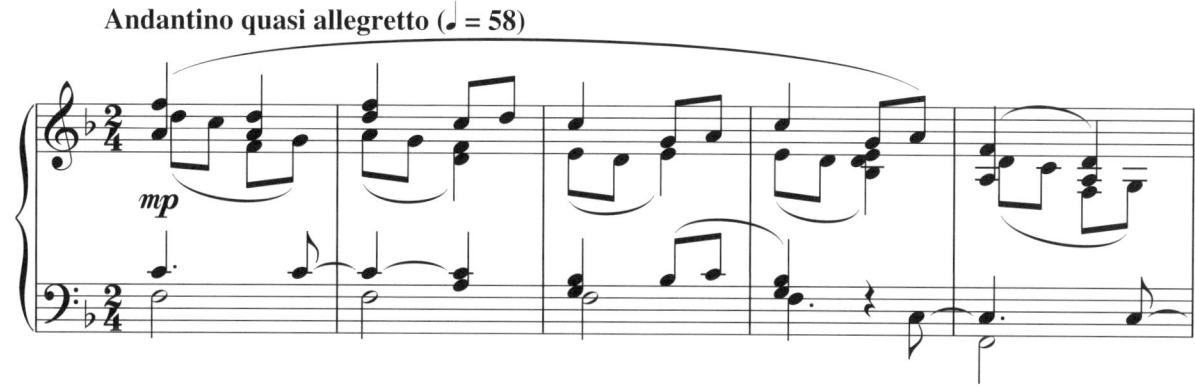

Dark brown is the riv-er, Gold-en is the sand. It

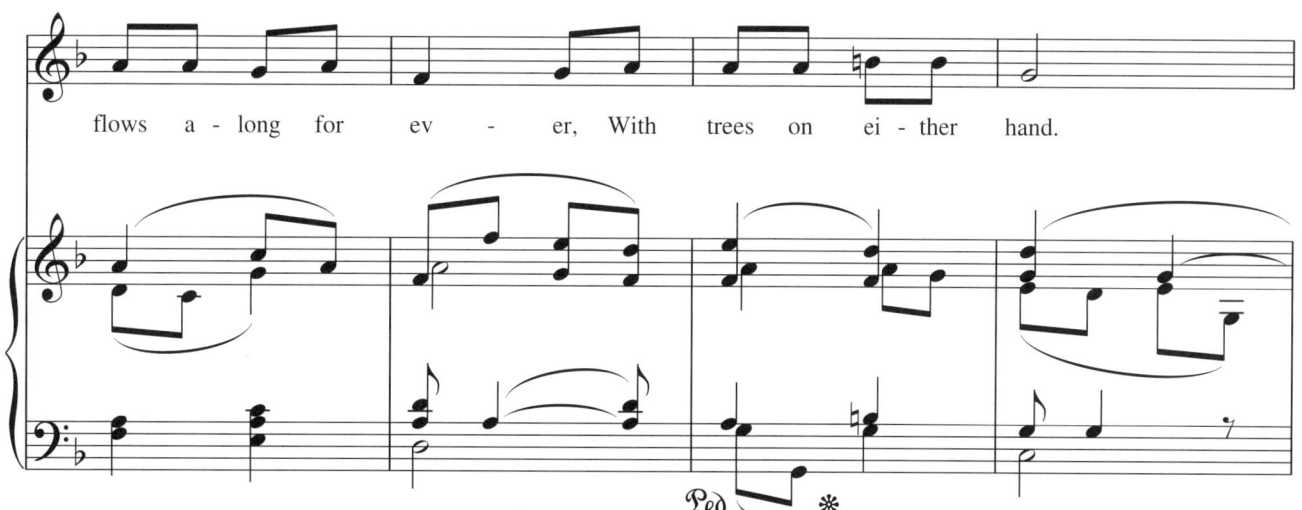

flows a-long for ev-er, With trees on ei-ther hand.

Copyright © 2003 by HAL LEONARD CORPORATION
International Copyright Secured   All Rights Reserved

44

To Walter Creighton

COME AWAY, DEATH
from Three Shakespeare Songs, Op. 6 (First Set)
original key

Words by
William Shakespeare
from *Twelfth Night*

Music by
Roger Quilter
Op. 6, No. 1

Copyright © 2003 by HAL LEONARD CORPORATION
International Copyright Secured   All Rights Reserved

To Walter Creighton

O MISTRESS MINE
from Three Shakespeare Songs, Op. 6 (First Set)
original key

Words by
William Shakespeare
from *Twelfth Night*

Music by
Roger Quilter
Op. 6, No. 2

Copyright © 2003 by HAL LEONARD CORPORATION
International Copyright Secured   All Rights Reserved

To Gervase Elwes

TO JULIA
Prelude

original key: D Major

Roger Quilter
Op. 8

Moderato tranquillo e con tenerezza (♩ = 69)

Copyright © 2003 by HAL LEONARD CORPORATION
International Copyright Secured   All Rights Reserved

I. The Bracelet
from *To Julia*
original key: D minor

Words by
Robert Herrick

Music by
Roger Quilter
Op. 8, No. 1

II. The Maiden Blush

from *To Julia*

original key: F Major

Words by Robert Herrick

Music by Roger Quilter
Op. 8, No. 2

Copyright © 2003 by HAL LEONARD CORPORATION
International Copyright Secured   All Rights Reserved

IV. The Night Piece

from *To Julia*

original key: C-sharp minor/D-flat Major

Words by
Robert Herrick

Music by
Roger Quilter
Op. 8, No. 4

Copyright © 2003 by HAL LEONARD CORPORATION
International Copyright Secured   All Rights Reserved

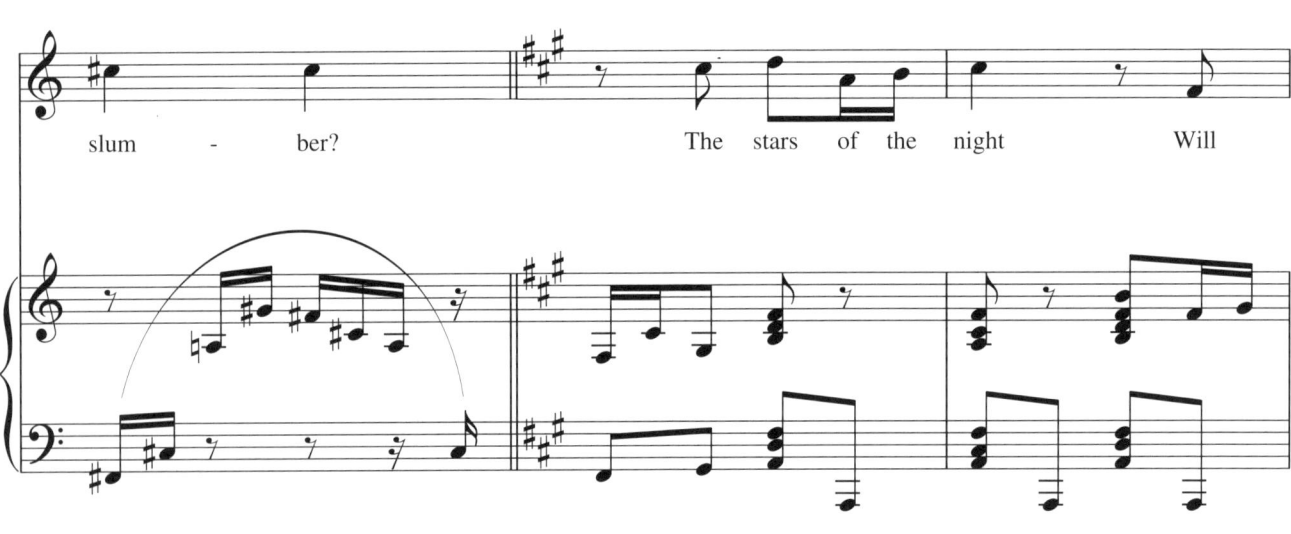

V. Julia's Hair
from *To Julia*
original key: A-flat Major

Words by
Robert Herrick

Music by
Roger Quilter
Op. 8, No. 5

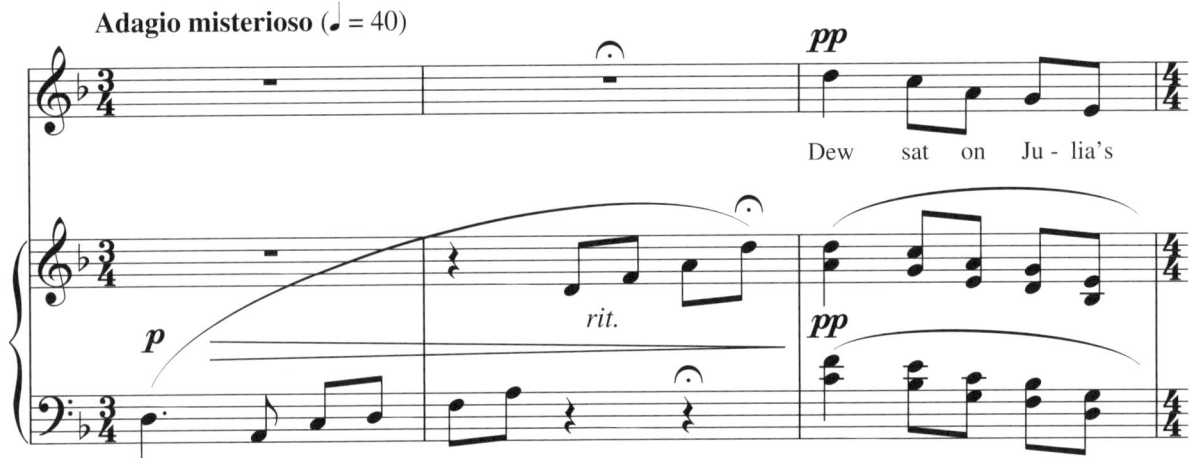

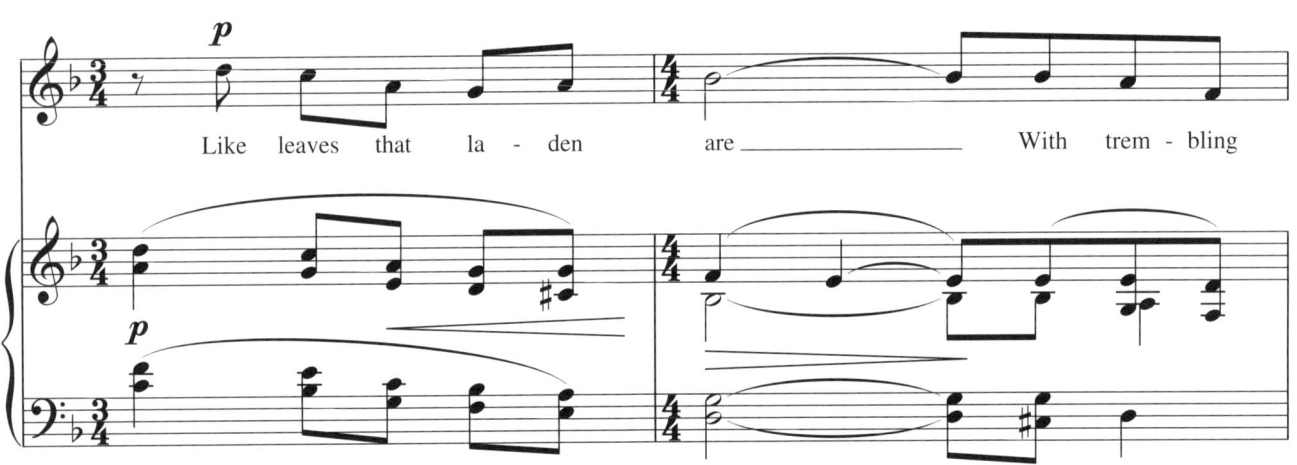

Copyright © 2003 by HAL LEONARD CORPORATION
International Copyright Secured   All Rights Reserved

Interlude

original key: a minor third higher

Music by
Roger Quilter
Op. 8

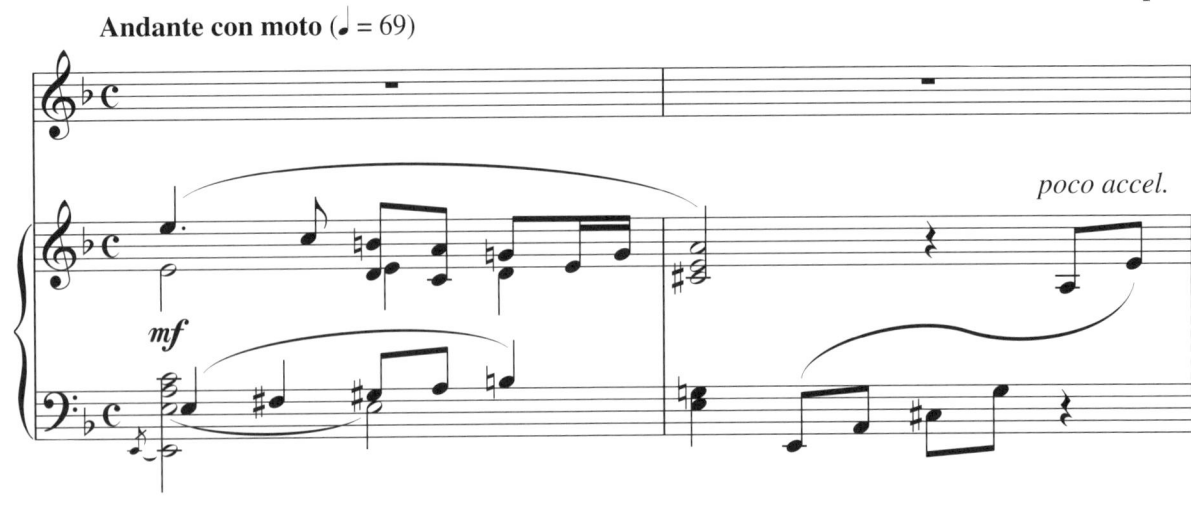

attacca, segue

Copyright © 2003 by HAL LEONARD CORPORATION
International Copyright Secured   All Rights Reserved

VI. Cherry Ripe

from *To Julia*
original key: F Major

Words by
Robert Herrick

Music by
Roger Quilter
Op. 8, No. 6

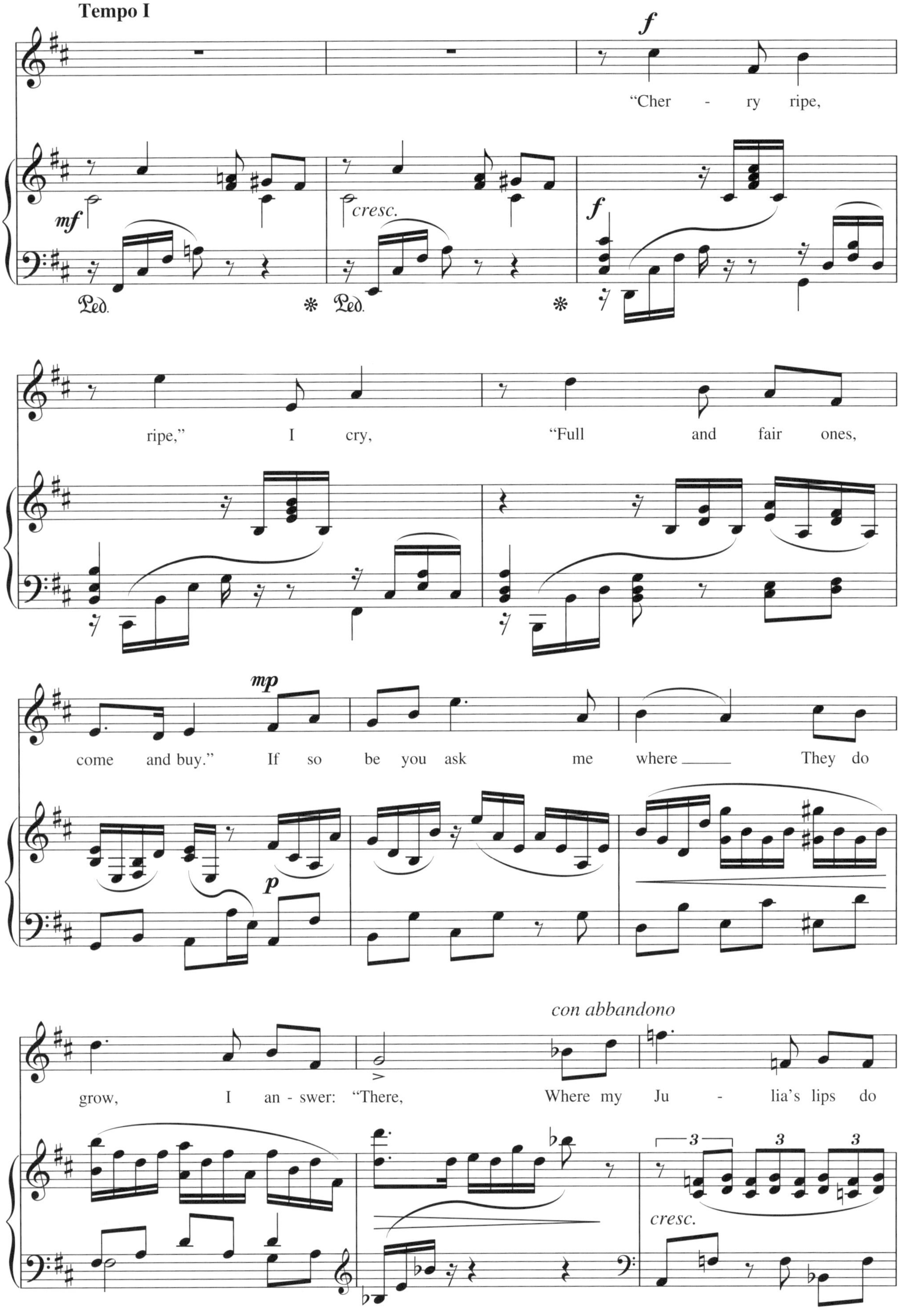
Tempo I
f
"Cher - ry ripe,
mf
cresc.
f
Ped.
Ped.
ripe," I cry, "Full and fair ones,
mp
come and buy." If so be you ask me where ___ They do
p
con abbandono
grow, I an - swer: "There, Where my Ju - lia's lips do
cresc.

To the memory of my friend, Mrs. Cary-Elwes

THE FAITHLESS SHEPHERDESS
from Seven Elizabethan Songs, Op. 12
original key: B-flat minor

Words Anonymous

Music by
Roger Quilter
Op. 12, No. 4

Copyright © 2003 by HAL LEONARD CORPORATION
International Copyright Secured   All Rights Reserved

To the memory of my friend, Mrs. Cary-Elwes

WEEP YOU NO MORE
from Seven Elizabethan Songs, Op. 12

original key: F minor

Words Anonymous

Music by
Roger Quilter
Op. 12, No. 1

To the memory of my friend, Mrs. Cary-Elwes

MY LIFE'S DELIGHT
from Seven Elizabethan Songs, Op. 12
original key: G Major

Words by
Thomas Campion

Music by
Roger Quilter
Op. 12, No. 2

Molto allegro con moto (♩ = 132)

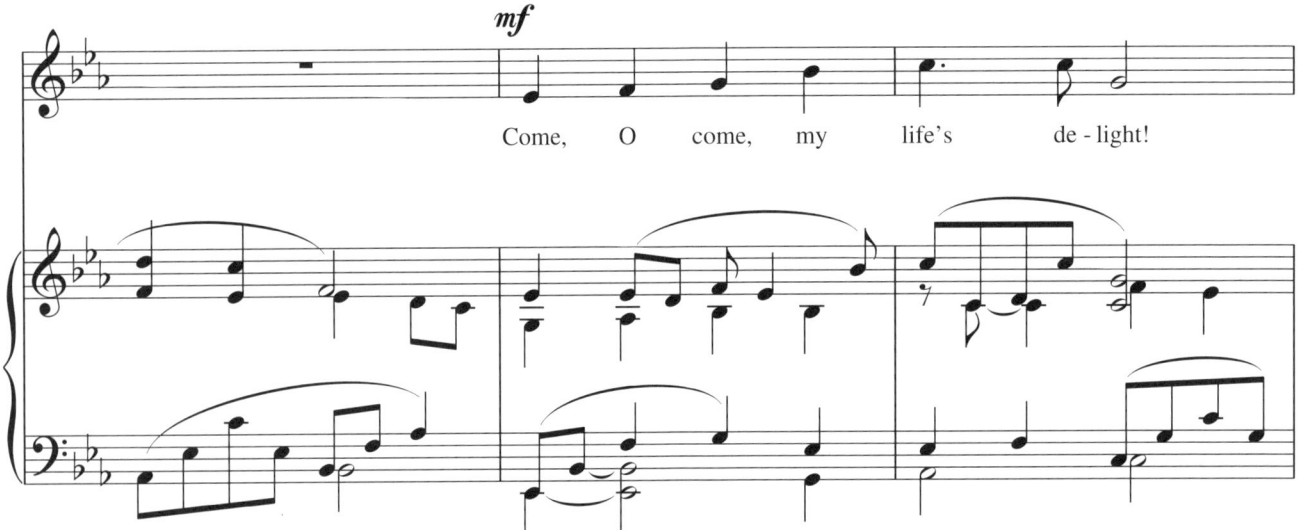

Come, O come, my life's de-light!

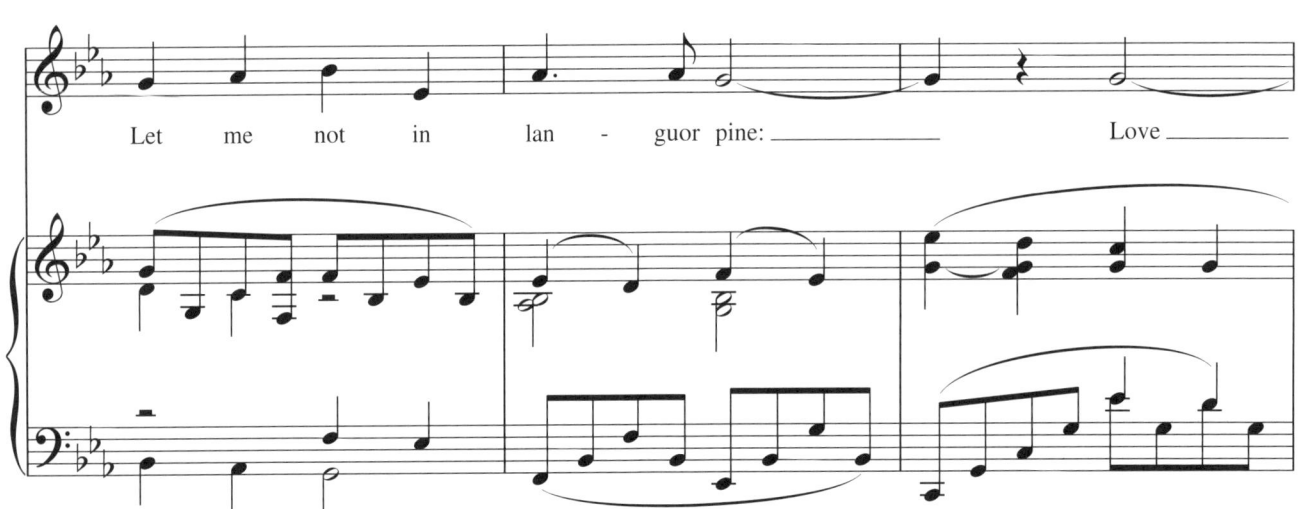

Let me not in lan- guor pine: _____ Love _____

Copyright © 2003 by HAL LEONARD CORPORATION
International Copyright Secured All Rights Reserved

98

To the memory of my friend, Mrs. Cary-Elwes

DAMASK ROSES
from Seven Elizabethan Songs, Op. 12
original key: D Major

Words Anonymous

Music by
Roger Quilter
Op. 12, No. 3

Copyright © 2003 by HAL LEONARD CORPORATION
International Copyright Secured   All Rights Reserved

To the memory of my friend, Mrs. Cary-Elwes

BROWN IS MY LOVE
from Seven Elizabethan Songs, Op. 12
original key: B-flat Major

Words Anonymous

Music by
Roger Quilter
Op. 12, No. 5

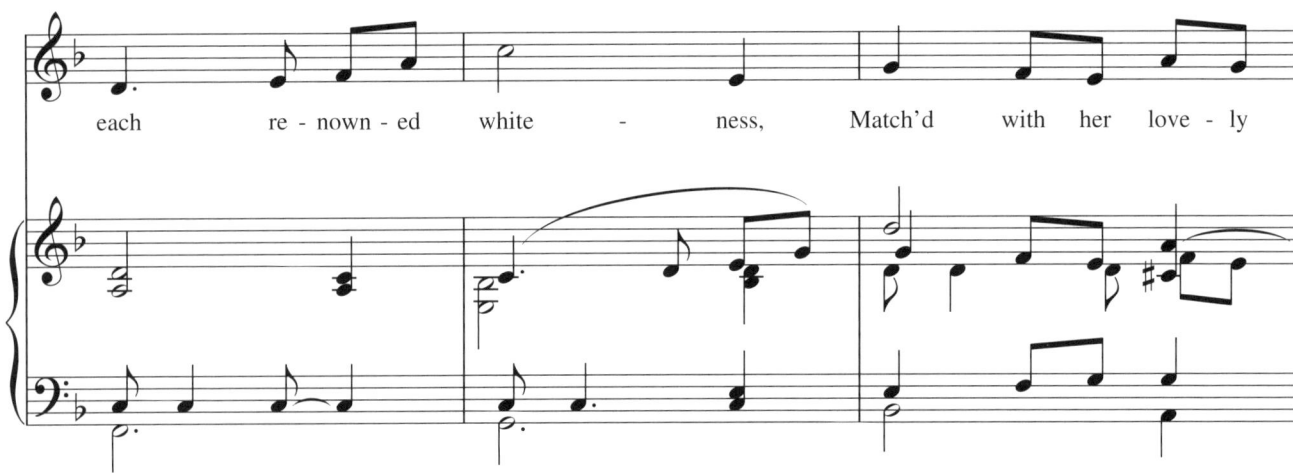

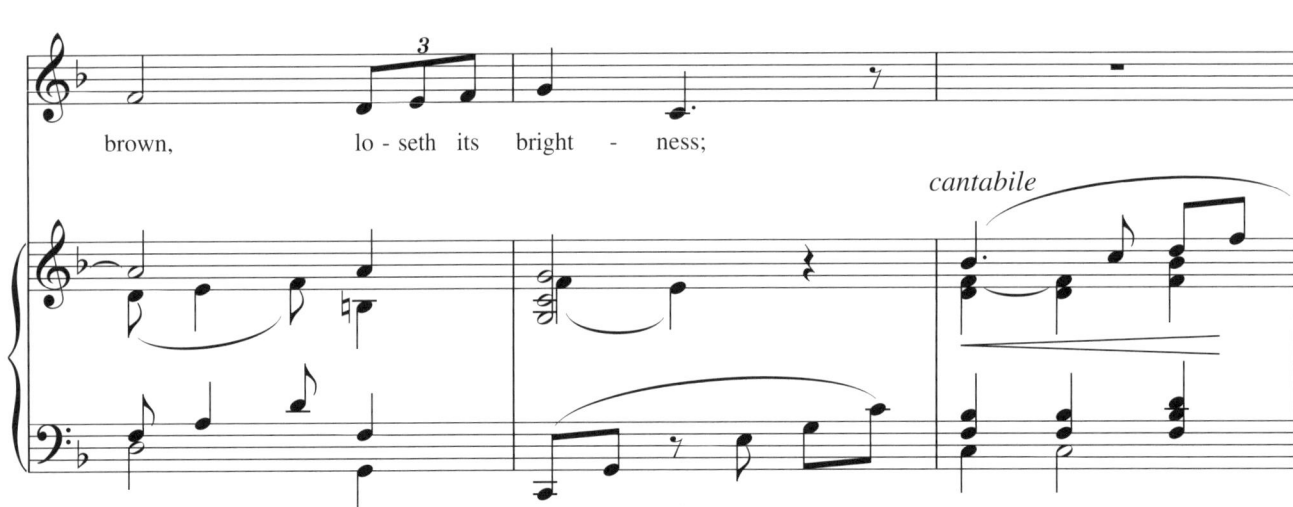

Copyright © 2003 by HAL LEONARD CORPORATION
International Copyright Secured   All Rights Reserved

102

To the memory of my friend, Mrs. Cary-Elwes

BY A FOUNTAINSIDE
from Seven Elizabethan Songs, Op. 12
original key: C-sharp minor

Words by
Ben Jonson

Music by
Roger Quilter
Op. 12, No. 6

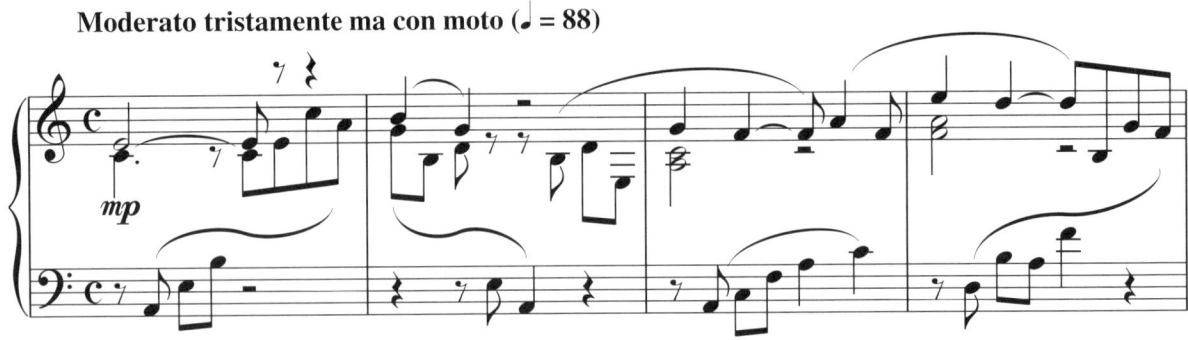

Slow, slow, fresh fount, keep time with my salt tears; Yet

slow - er, yet: O faint-ly, gen-tle springs:

Copyright © 2003 by HAL LEONARD CORPORATION
International Copyright Secured   All Rights Reserved

106

To the memory of my friend, Mrs. Cary-Elwes

FAIR HOUSE OF JOY
from Seven Elizabethan Songs, Op. 12

original key: D-flat Major

Words Anonymous

Music by
Roger Quilter
Op. 12, No. 7

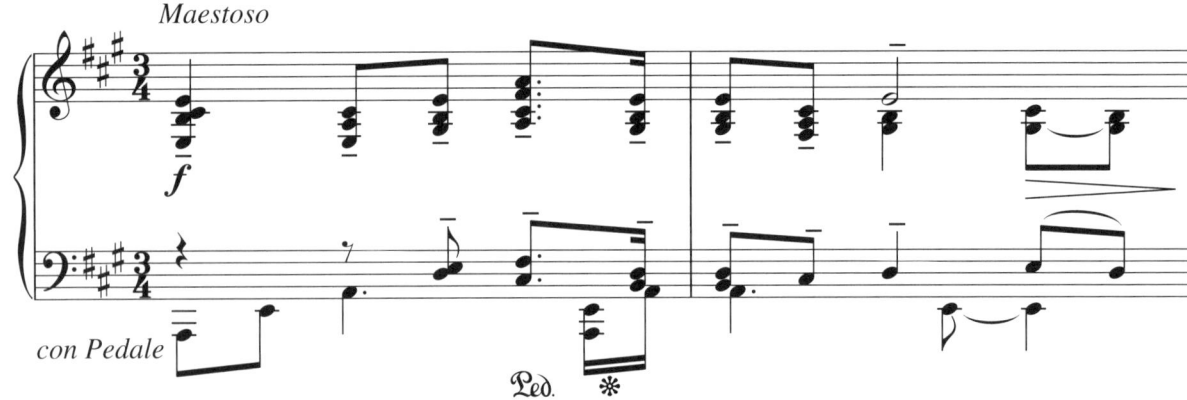

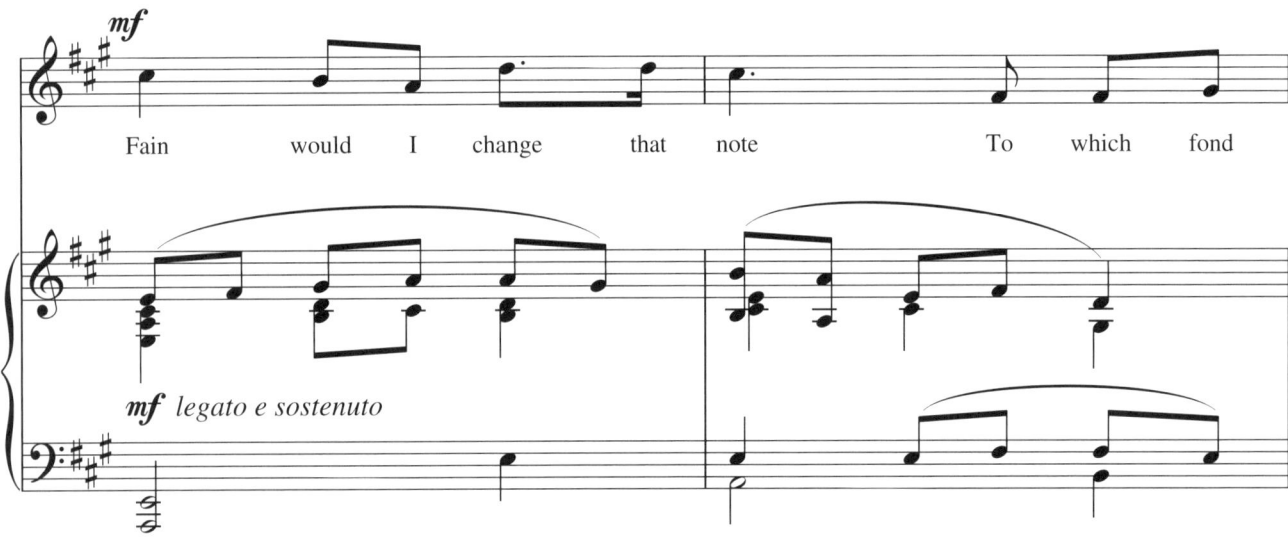

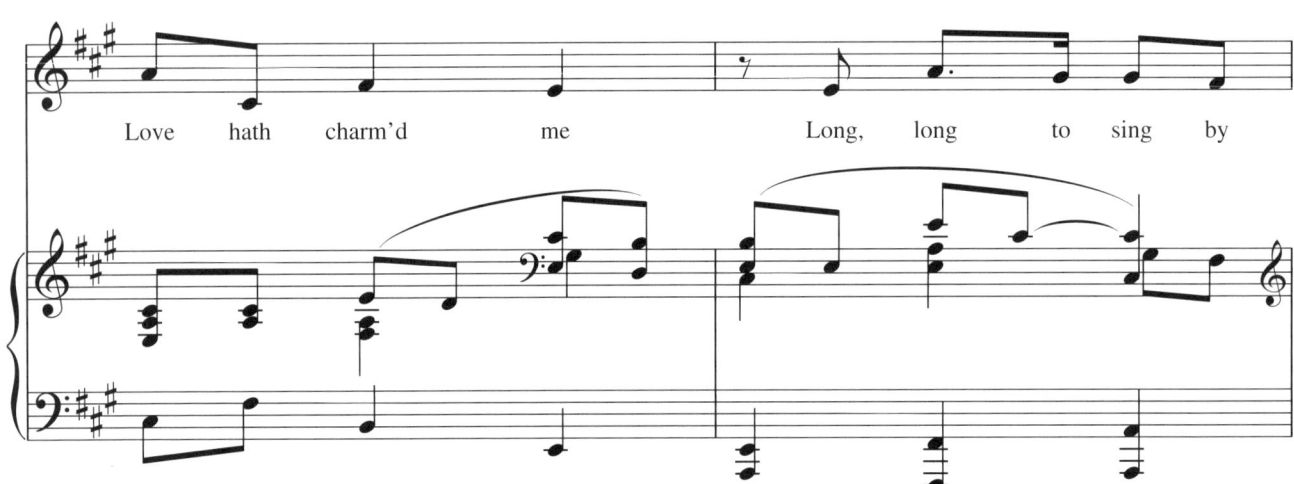

Copyright © 2003 by HAL LEONARD CORPORATION
International Copyright Secured   All Rights Reserved

To Robin and Aimée Legge

AUTUMN EVENING
from Four Songs, Op. 14
original key

Words by
Arthur Maquarie

Music by
Roger Quilter
Op. 14, No. 1

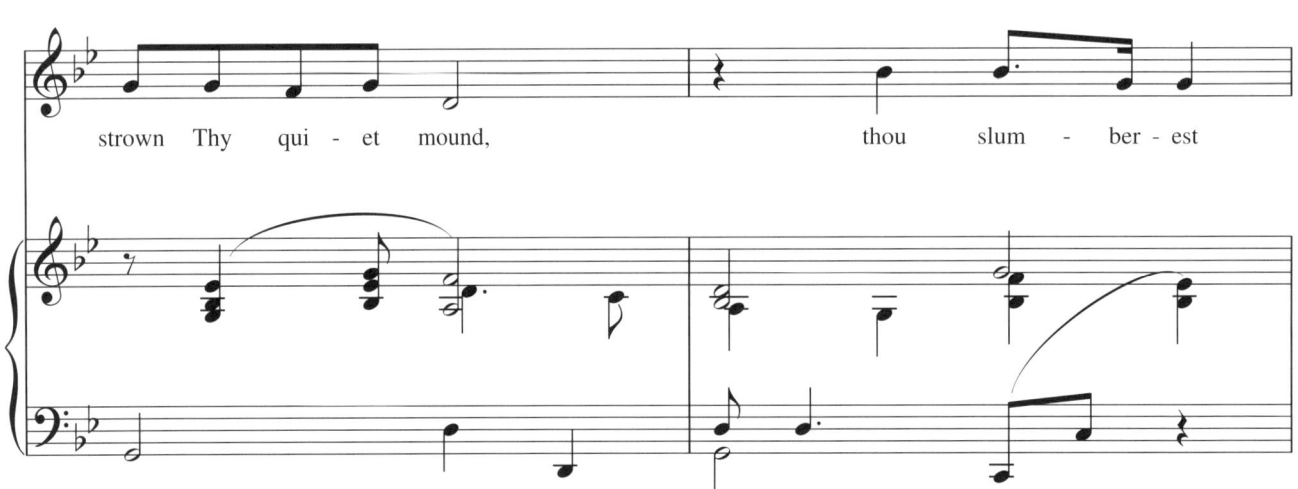

Copyright © 2003 by HAL LEONARD CORPORATION
International Copyright Secured   All Rights Reserved

To Robin and Aimée Legge

APRIL

from Four Songs, Op. 14

original key: A-flat Major

Words by
William Watson

Music by
Roger Quilter
Op. 14, No. 2

Copyright © 2003 by HAL LEONARD CORPORATION
International Copyright Secured   All Rights Reserved

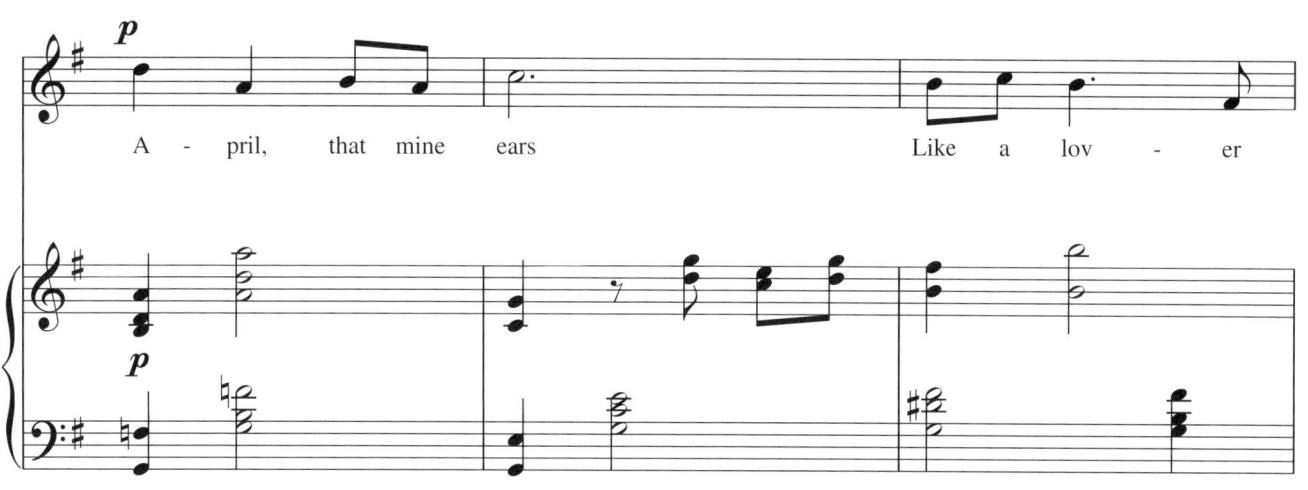

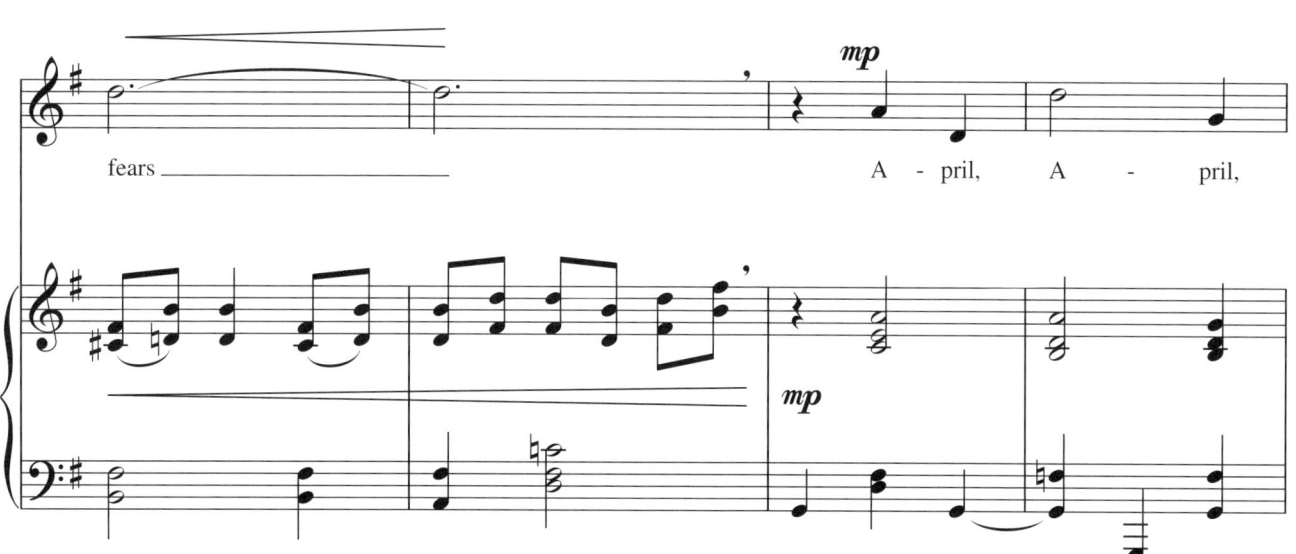

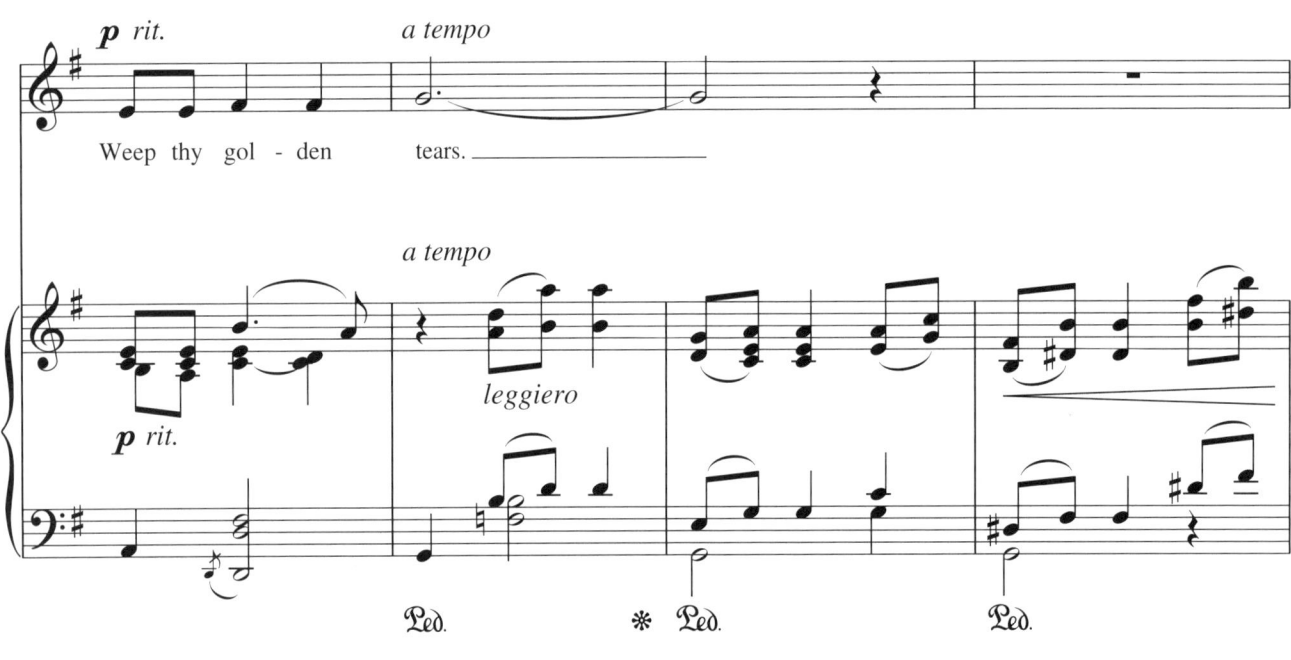
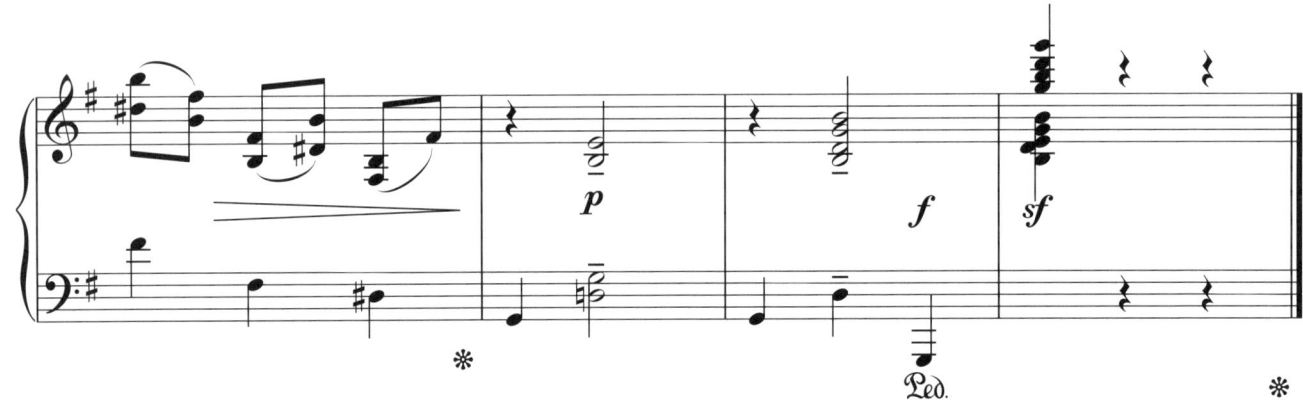

Words by
W.E. Henley

To Robin and Aimée Legge
A LAST YEAR'S ROSE
from Four Songs, Op. 14
original key: D-flat Major

Music by
Roger Quilter
Op. 14, No. 3

Copyright © 2003 by HAL LEONARD CORPORATION
International Copyright Secured All Rights Reserved

121

To Robin and Aimée Legge

SONG OF THE BLACKBIRD
from Four Songs, Op. 14
original key: C Major

Words by
W.E. Henley

Music by
Roger Quilter
Op. 14, No. 4

Copyright © 2003 by HAL LEONARD CORPORATION
International Copyright Secured   All Rights Reserved

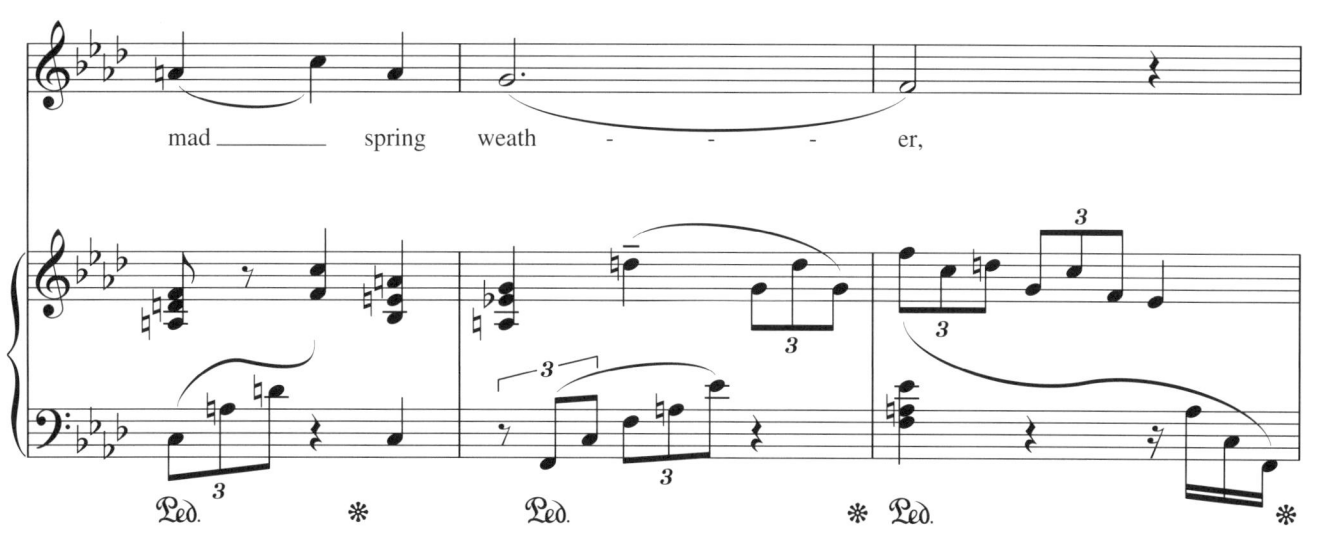

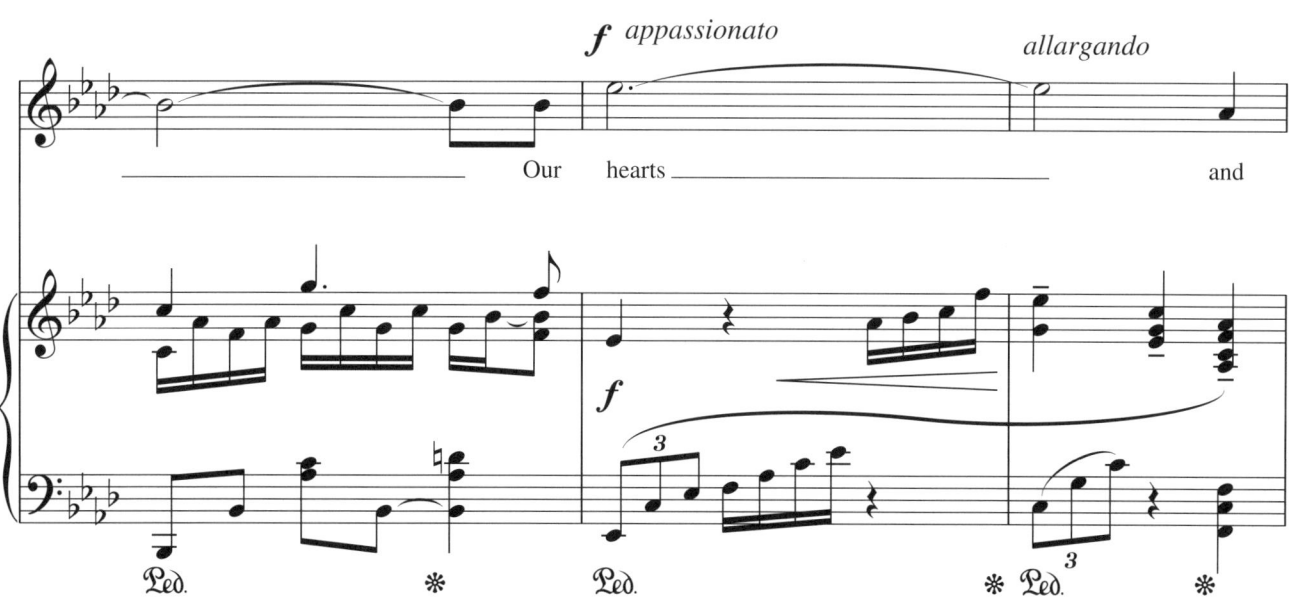

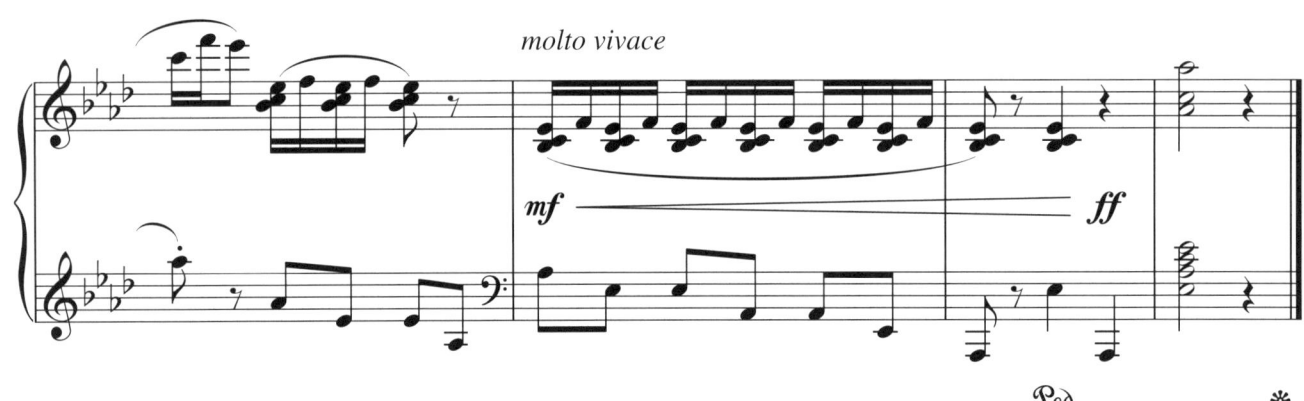

to H. Plunket Greene

WHERE BE YOU GOING?

from Six Songs, Op. 18

original key

Words by
John Keats

Music by
Roger Quilter
Op. 18, No. 2

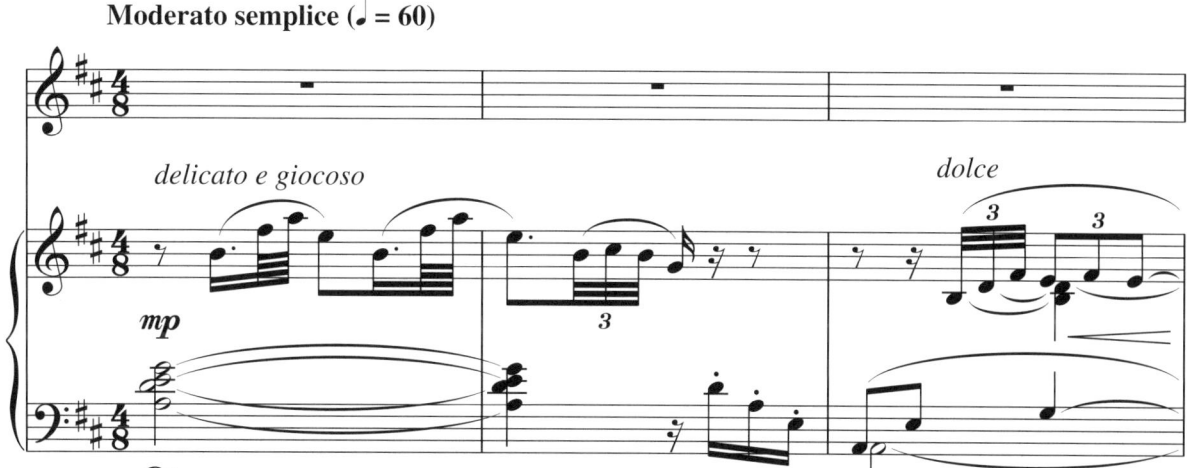

Where be you going, you Dev-on maid? And

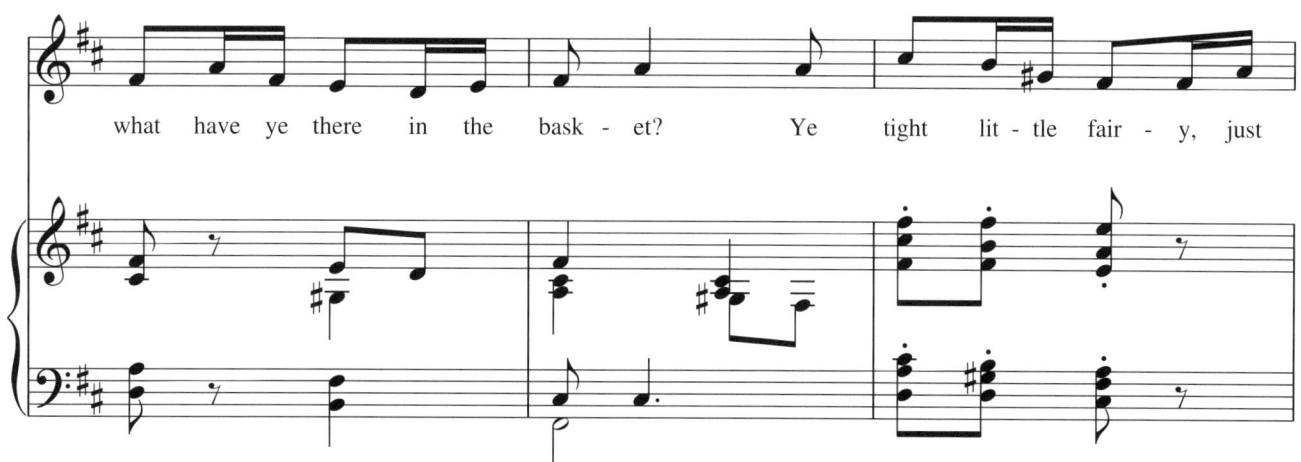

what have ye there in the bask-et? Ye tight lit-tle fair-y, just

Copyright © 2003 by HAL LEONARD CORPORATION
International Copyright Secured   All Rights Reserved

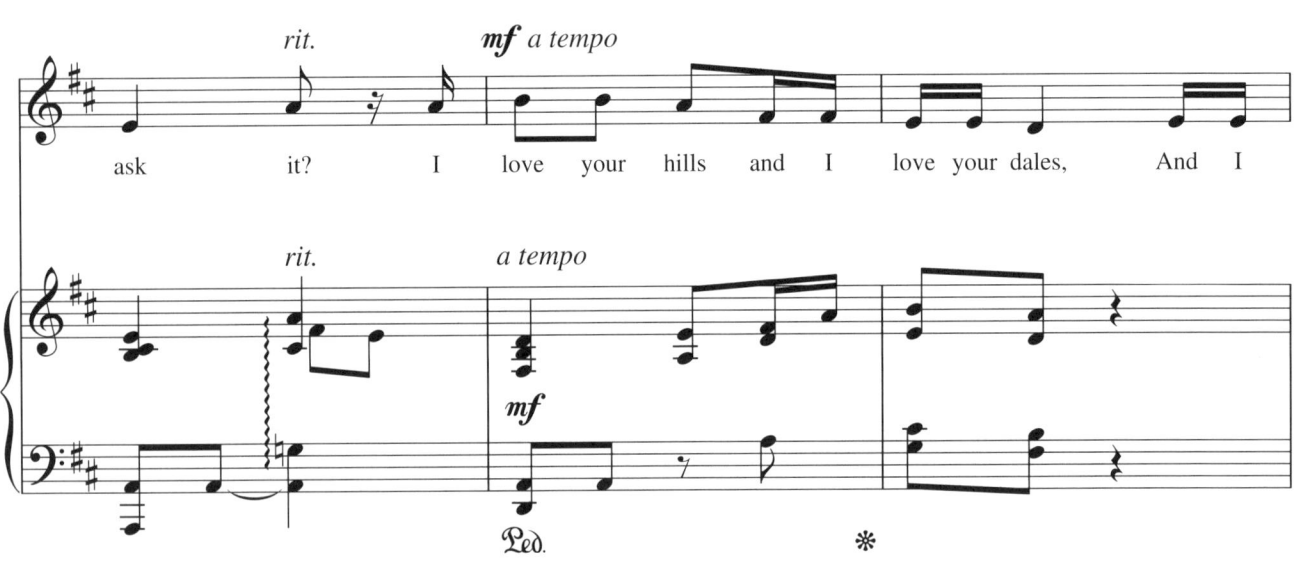
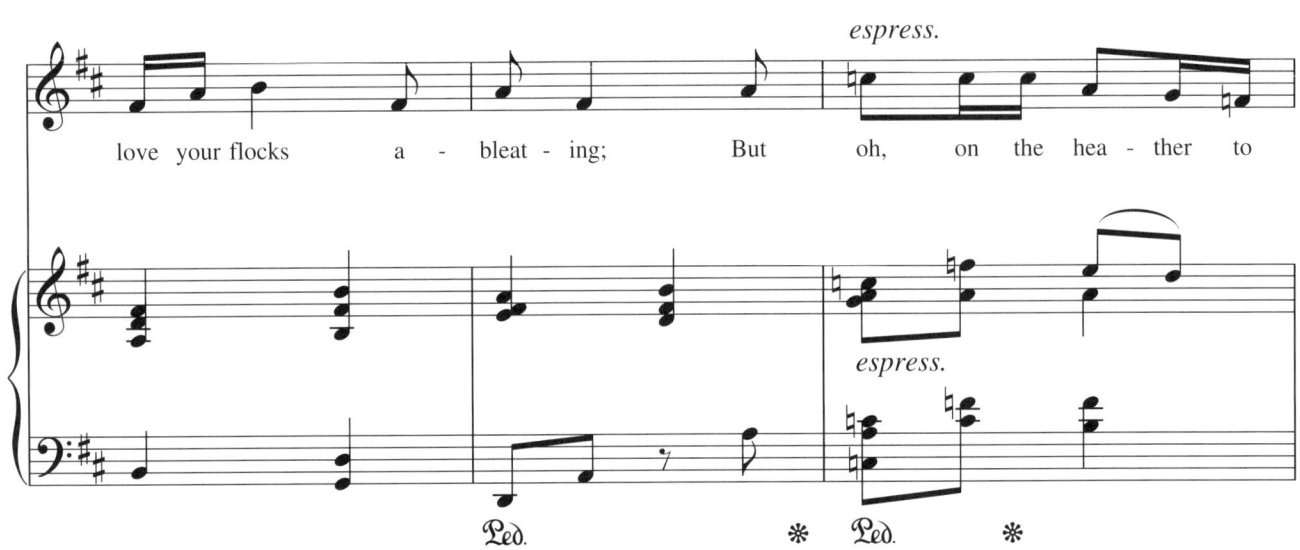

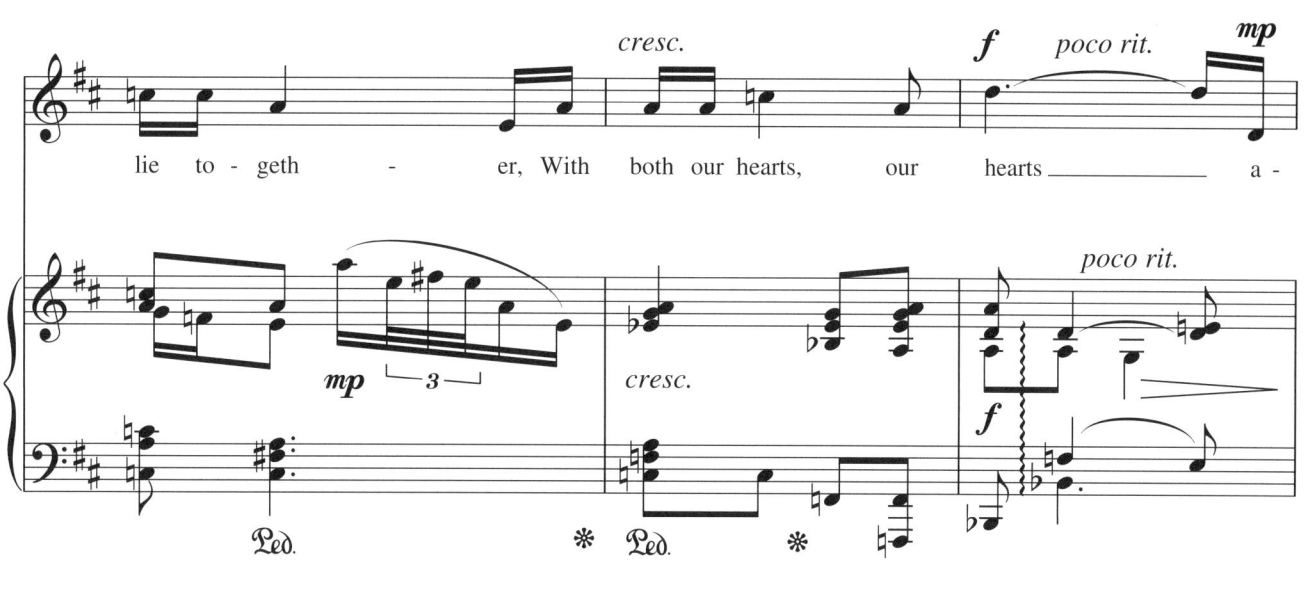
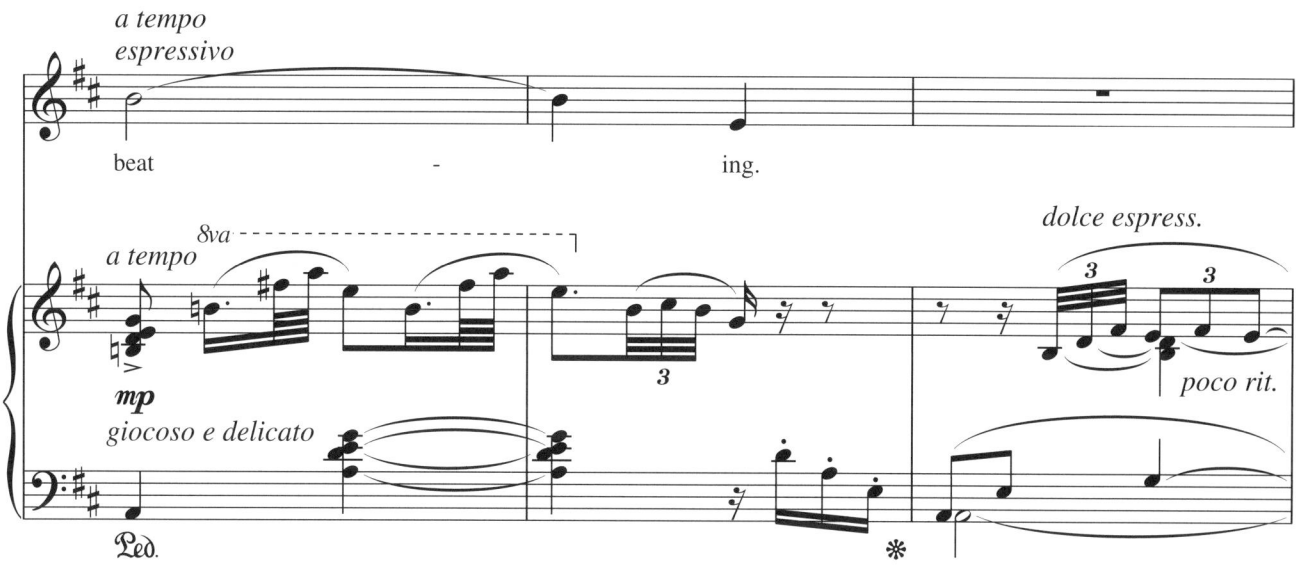
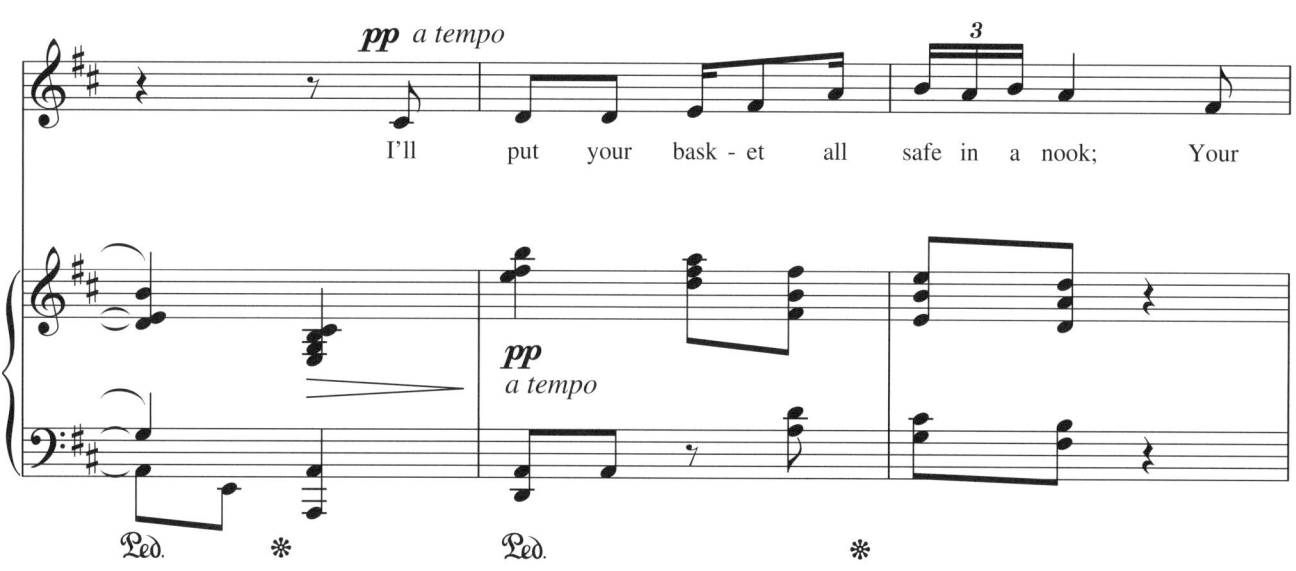

133

to Frederic Austin
THE JOCUND DANCE
from Six Songs, Op. 18
original key

Words by
William Blake

Music by
Roger Quilter
Op. 18, No. 3

Copyright © 2003 by HAL LEONARD CORPORATION
International Copyright Secured   All Rights Reserved

THE SPRING IS AT THE DOOR

to Madame Kirkby Lunn

from Six Songs, Op. 18

original key: D Major

Words by
Nora Hopper

Music by
Roger Quilter
Op. 18, No. 4

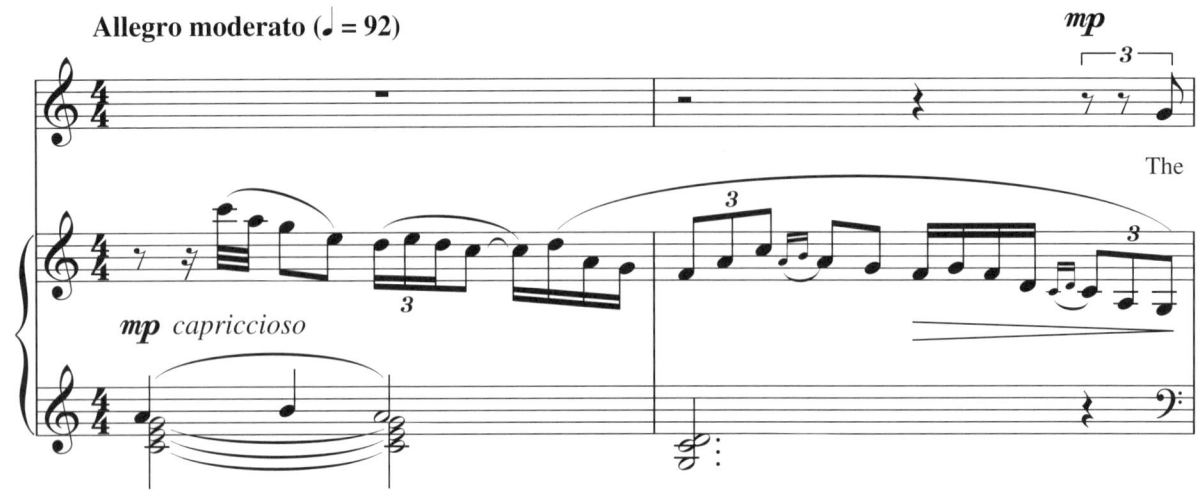

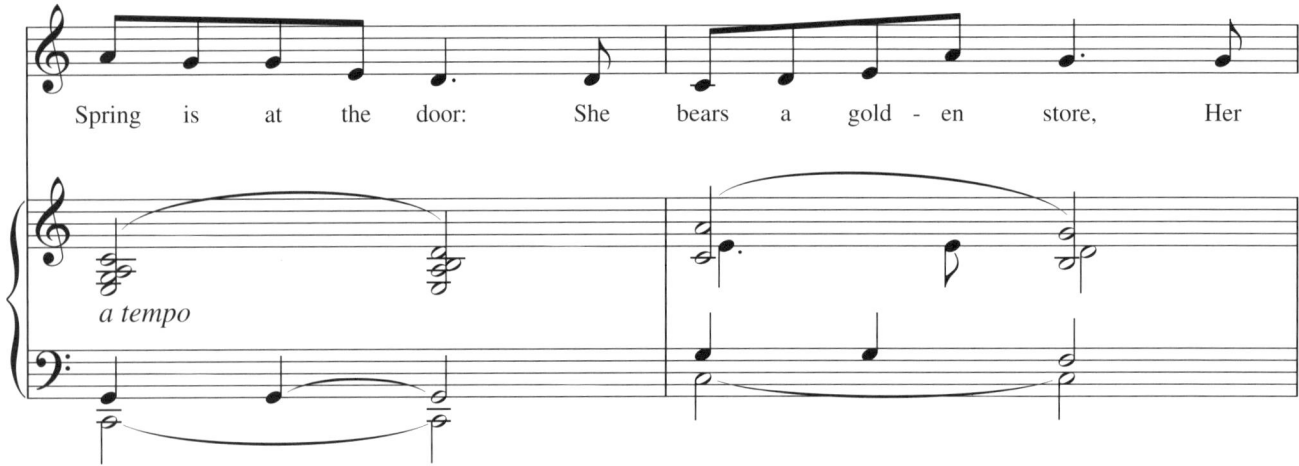

Spring is at the door: She bears a gold-en store, Her

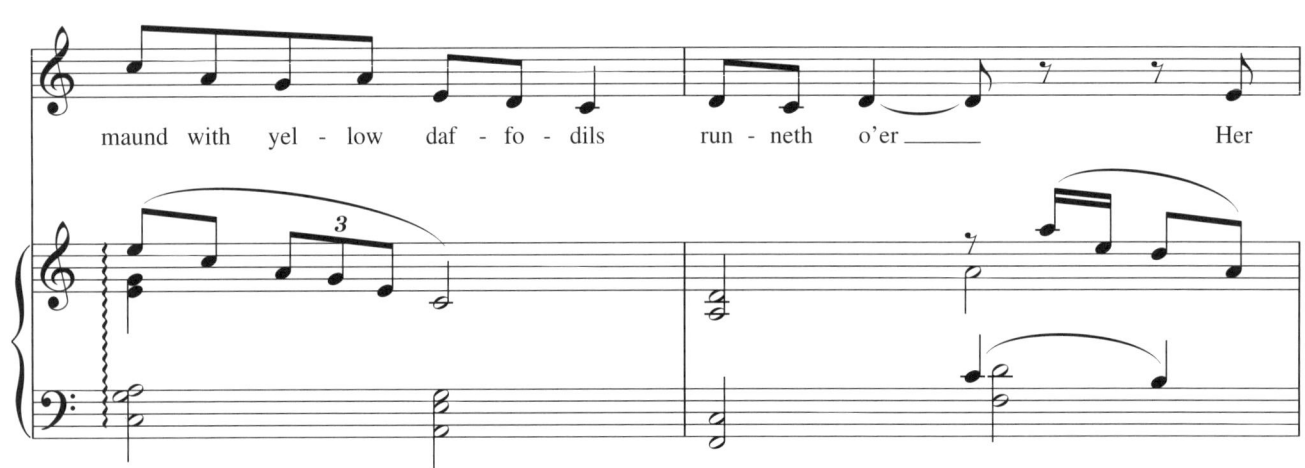

maund with yel-low daf-fo-dils run-neth o'er___ Her

Copyright © 2003 by HAL LEONARD CORPORATION
International Copyright Secured   All Rights Reserved

142

To Miss Muriel Foster

THROUGH THE SUNNY GARDEN
from Two September Songs, Op. 18
original key

Words by
Mary Coleridge

Music by
Roger Quilter
Op. 18, No. 5

Andante moderato (♩ = 42)

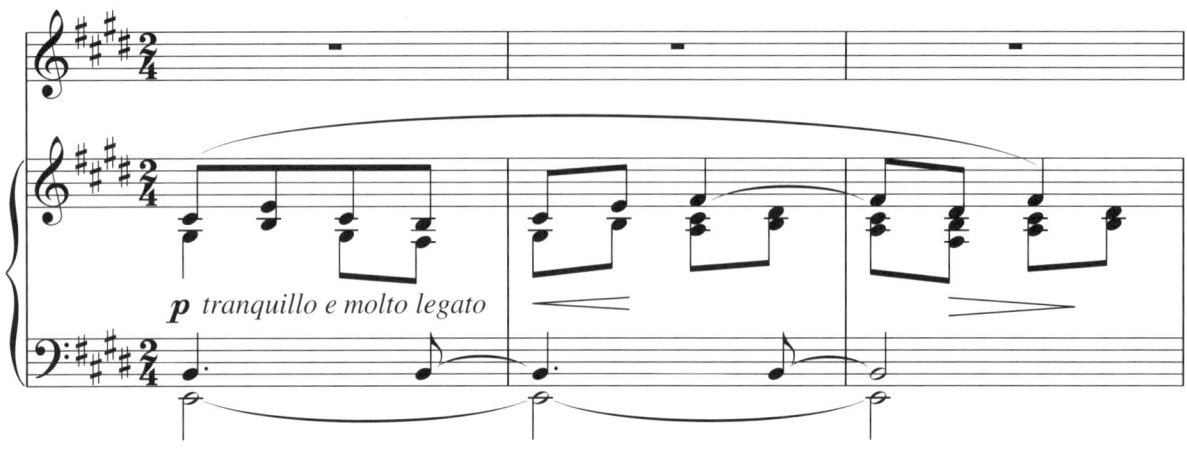

p tranquillo e molto legato

Through the sun-ny gar-den The hum-mimg bees are still;

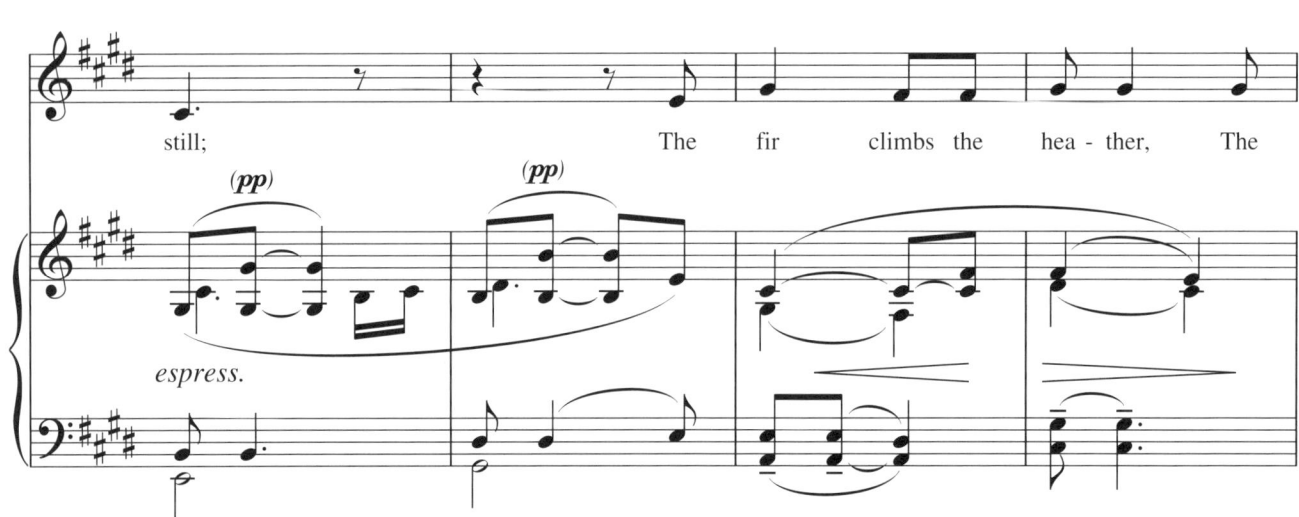

The fir climbs the hea-ther, The

espress.

Copyright © 2003 by HAL LEONARD CORPORATION
International Copyright Secured   All Rights Reserved

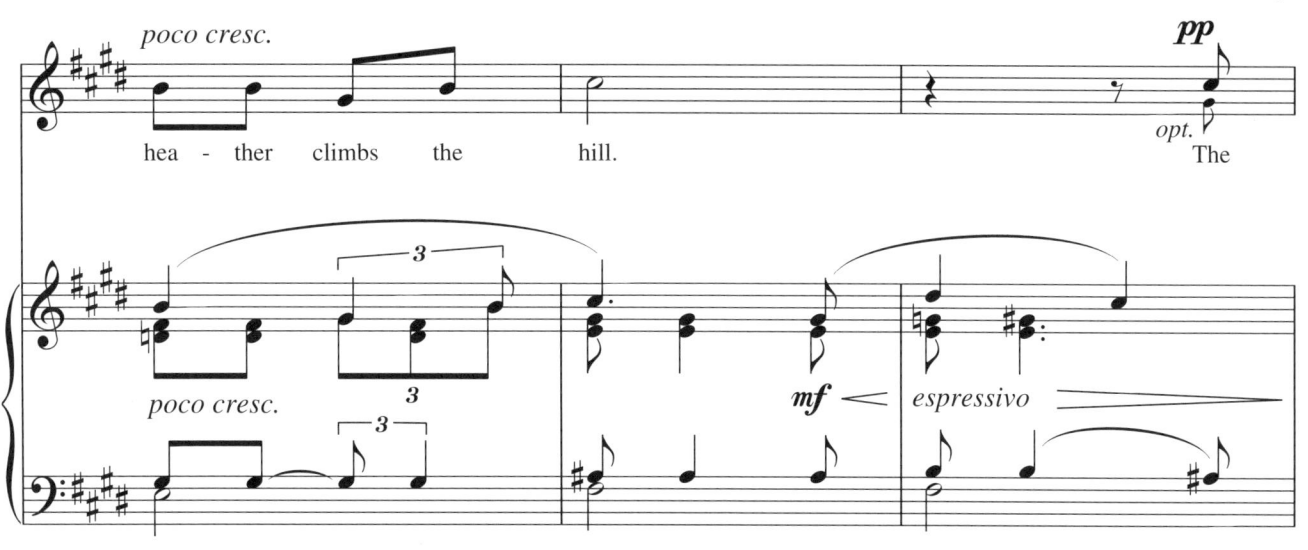

To Miss Muriel Foster

THE VALLEY AND THE HILL
from Two September Songs, Op. 18

original key

Words by
Mary Coleridge

Music by
Roger Quilter
Op. 18, No. 6

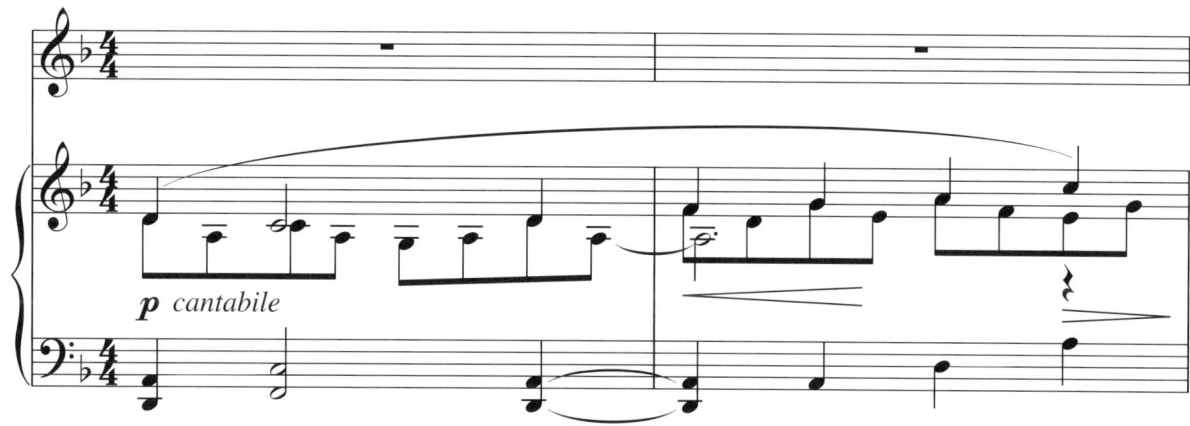

O the high valley, the little low hill. And the cornfield over the

sea, ___ The wind that rages and then lies still, And the

Copyright © 2003 by HAL LEONARD CORPORATION
International Copyright Secured   All Rights Reserved

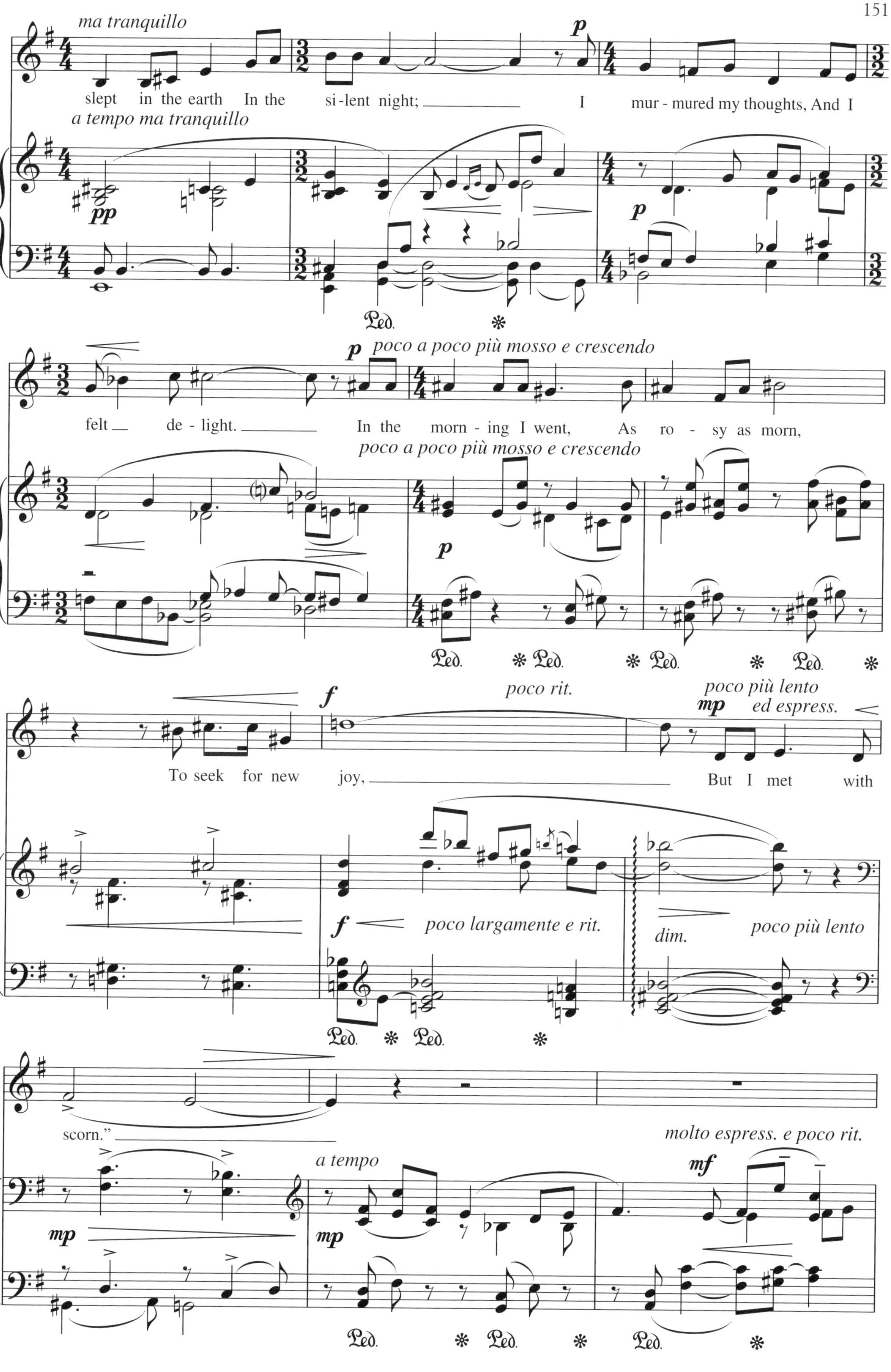
ma tranquillo
slept in the earth In the si-lent night; I mur-mured my thoughts, And I
a tempo ma tranquillo
felt de-light. In the morn-ing I went, As ro-sy as morn,
poco a poco più mosso e crescendo
poco rit.
poco più lento ed espress.
To seek for new joy, But I met with
poco largamente e rit.
dim.
poco più lento
scorn."
a tempo
molto espress. e poco rit.

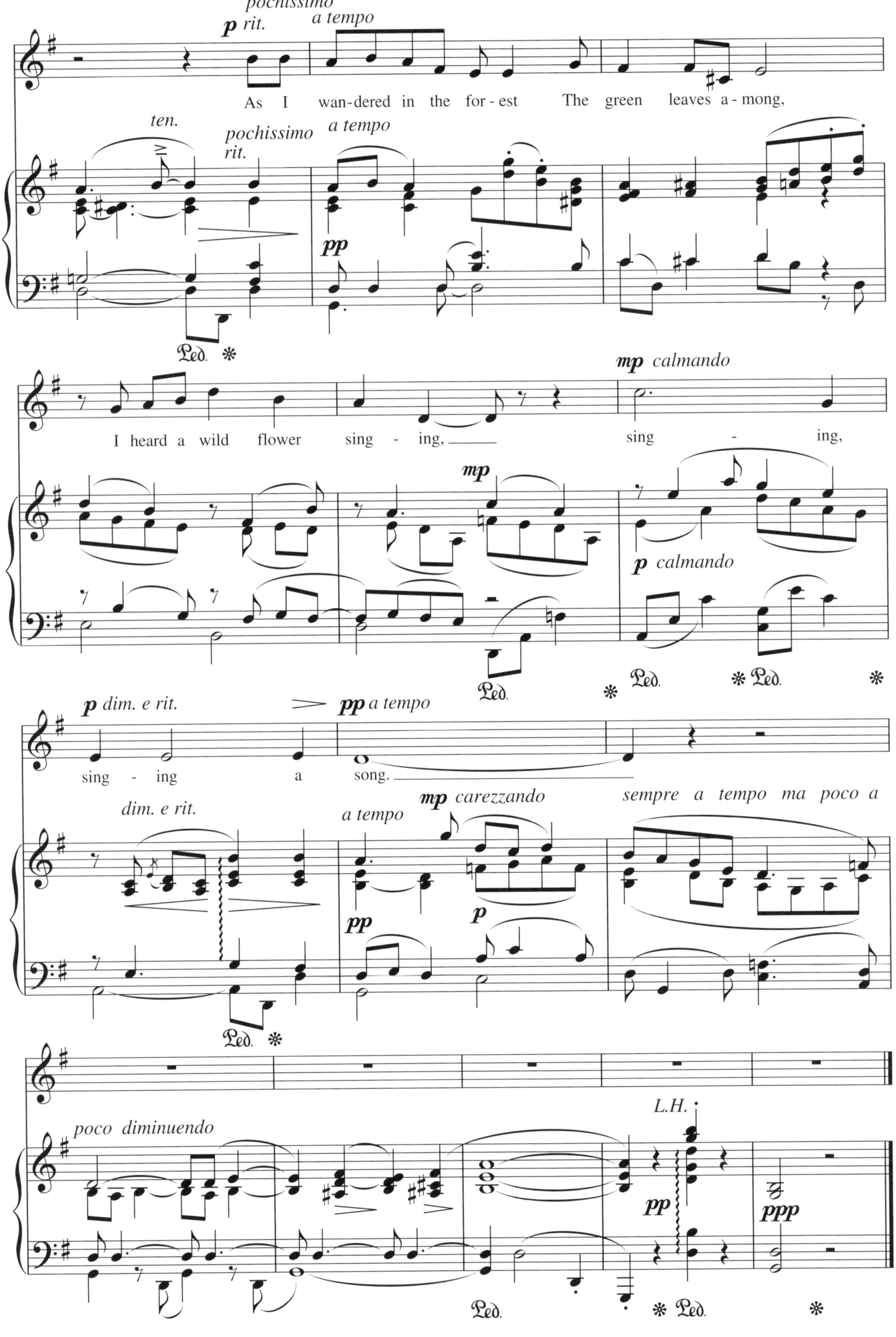
pochissimo
p rit.
a tempo
As I wan-dered in the for-est The green leaves a-mong,
ten.
pochissimo rit.
a tempo
pp
Ped. *
mp calmando
I heard a wild flower sing - ing, sing - ing,
mp
p calmando
Ped. * Ped. * Ped. *
p dim. e rit.
pp a tempo
sing - ing a song.
dim. e rit.
a tempo
mp carezzando
sempre a tempo ma poco a
pp
p
Ped. *
poco diminuendo
L.H.
pp
ppp
Ped. * Ped. *

156

To Monica Harrison

I WILL GO WITH MY FATHER A-PLOUGHING

from Three Pastoral Songs, Op. 22

original key

Words by
Joseph Campbell

Music by
Roger Quilter
Op. 22, No. 1

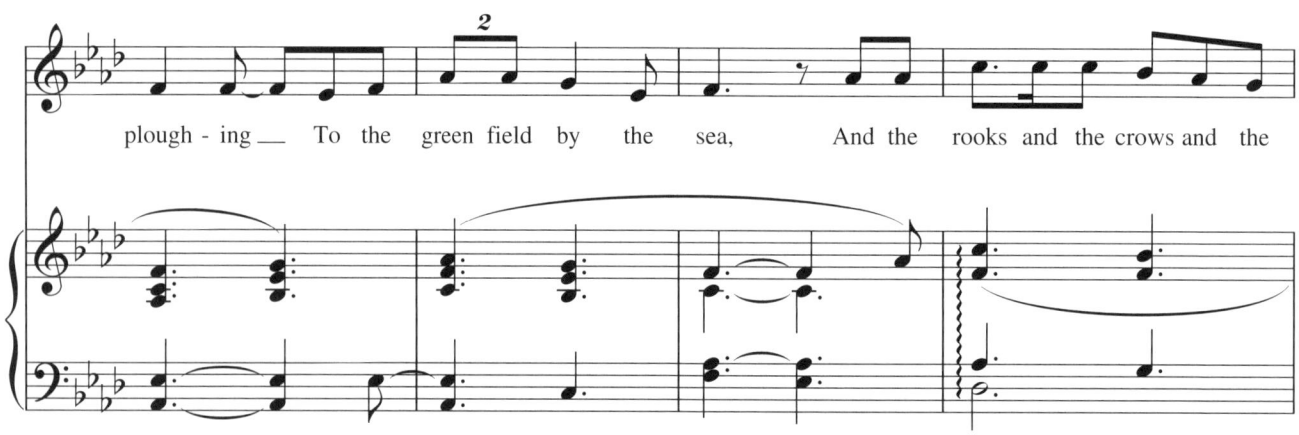

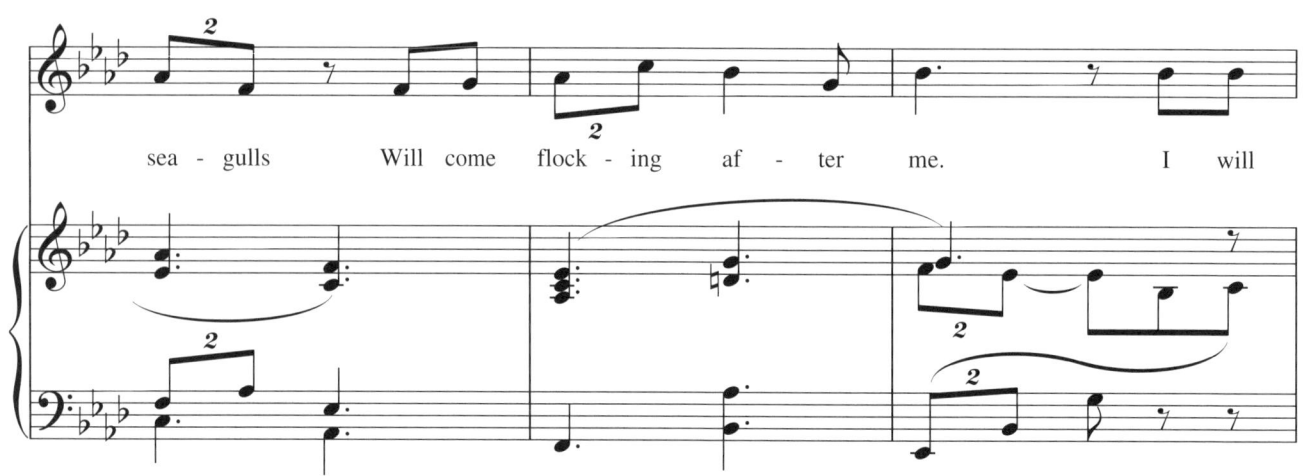

Copyright © 2003 by HAL LEONARD CORPORATION
International Copyright Secured   All Rights Reserved

To Monica Harrison

CHERRY VALLEY
from Three Pastoral Songs, Op. 22
original key

Words by
Joseph Campbell

Music by
Roger Quilter
Op. 22, No. 2

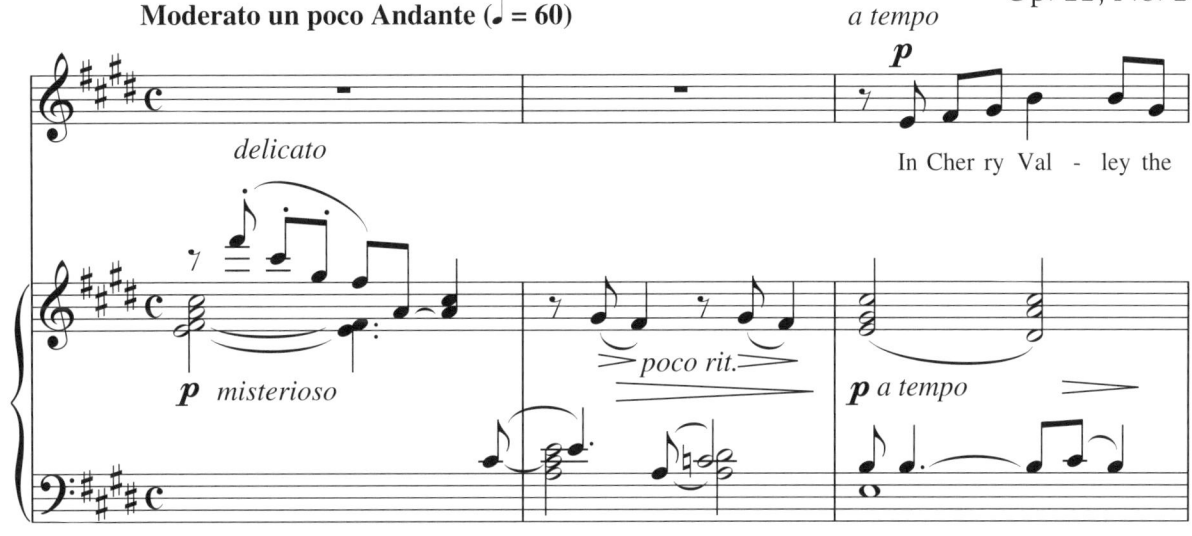

Copyright © 2003 by HAL LEONARD CORPORATION
International Copyright Secured   All Rights Reserved

To Monica Harrison

I WISH AND I WISH
from Three Pastoral Songs, Op. 22

original key

Words by
Joseph Campbell

Music by
Roger Quilter
Op. 22, No. 3

I wish and I wish And I wish I were A gold-en bee In the

blue of the air, Wing-ing my way At the mouth of day To the

Copyright © 2003 by HAL LEONARD CORPORATION
International Copyright Secured   All Rights Reserved

*Loch-ciuin-ban—"The fair, calm lake."

*Magh-meala—"The plain of honey"

168

UNDER THE GREENWOOD TREE
To Walter Creighton
from Five Shakespeare Songs, Op. 23 (Second Set)
original key

Words by
William Shakespeare
from *As You Like It*

Music by
Roger Quilter
Op. 23, No. 2

Copyright © 2003 by HAL LEONARD CORPORATION
International Copyright Secured   All Rights Reserved

FEAR NO MORE THE HEAT O' THE SUN

To the memory of Robin Hollway

from Five Shakespeare Songs, Op. 23 (Second Set)

original key

Words by William Shakespeare
from *Cymbeline*

Music by Roger Quilter
Op. 23, No. 1

Fear no more the heat o' the sun,
Nor the furious winter's rages;
Thou thy worldly task hast done,
Home art gone, and ta'en thy wages:
Golden lads and girls all must,
As chimney sweepers, come to dust.

Copyright © 2003 by HAL LEONARD CORPORATION
International Copyright Secured All Rights Reserved

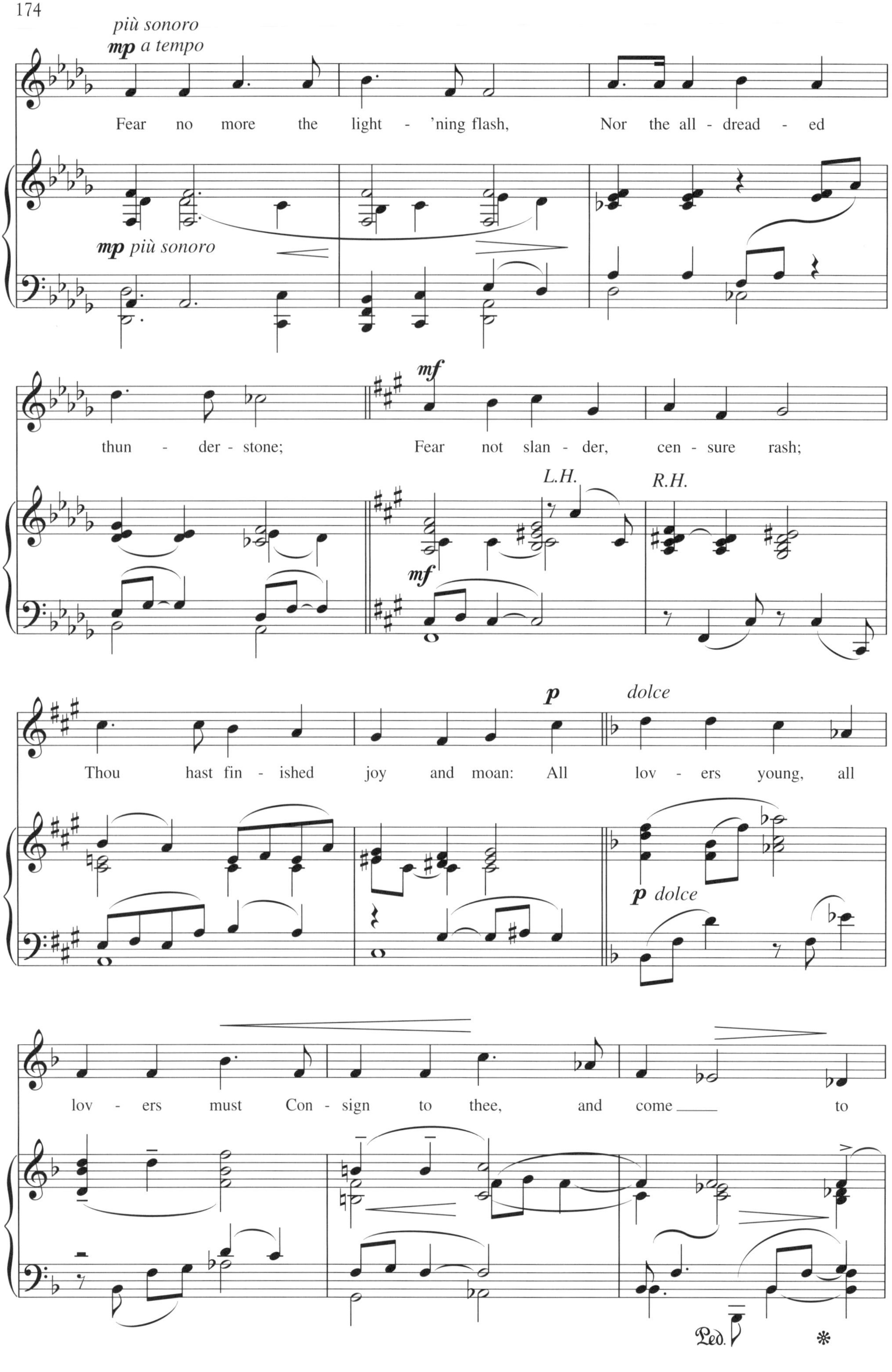
più sonoro
mp a tempo
Fear no more the light - 'ning flash, Nor the all - dread - ed
mp più sonoro
thun - der - stone; Fear not slan - der, cen - sure rash;
mf
L.H.
R.H.
Thou hast fin - ished joy and moan: All lov - ers young, all
p
dolce
p dolce
lov - ers must Con - sign to thee, and come to
Ped.

HEY, HO, THE WIND AND THE RAIN

To Walter Creighton

from Five Shakespeare Songs, Op. 23 (Second Set)

original key

Words by
William Shakespeare
from *Twelfth Night*

Music by
Roger Quilter
Op. 23, No. 5

Copyright © 2003 by HAL LEONARD CORPORATION
International Copyright Secured   All Rights Reserved

To Louis and Dinah de Glehn

OVER THE LAND IS APRIL
from Two Songs, Op. 26
original key

Words by
Robert Louis Stevenson

Music by
Roger Quilter
Op. 26, No. 2

Copyright © 2003 by HAL LEONARD CORPORATION
International Copyright Secured   All Rights Reserved

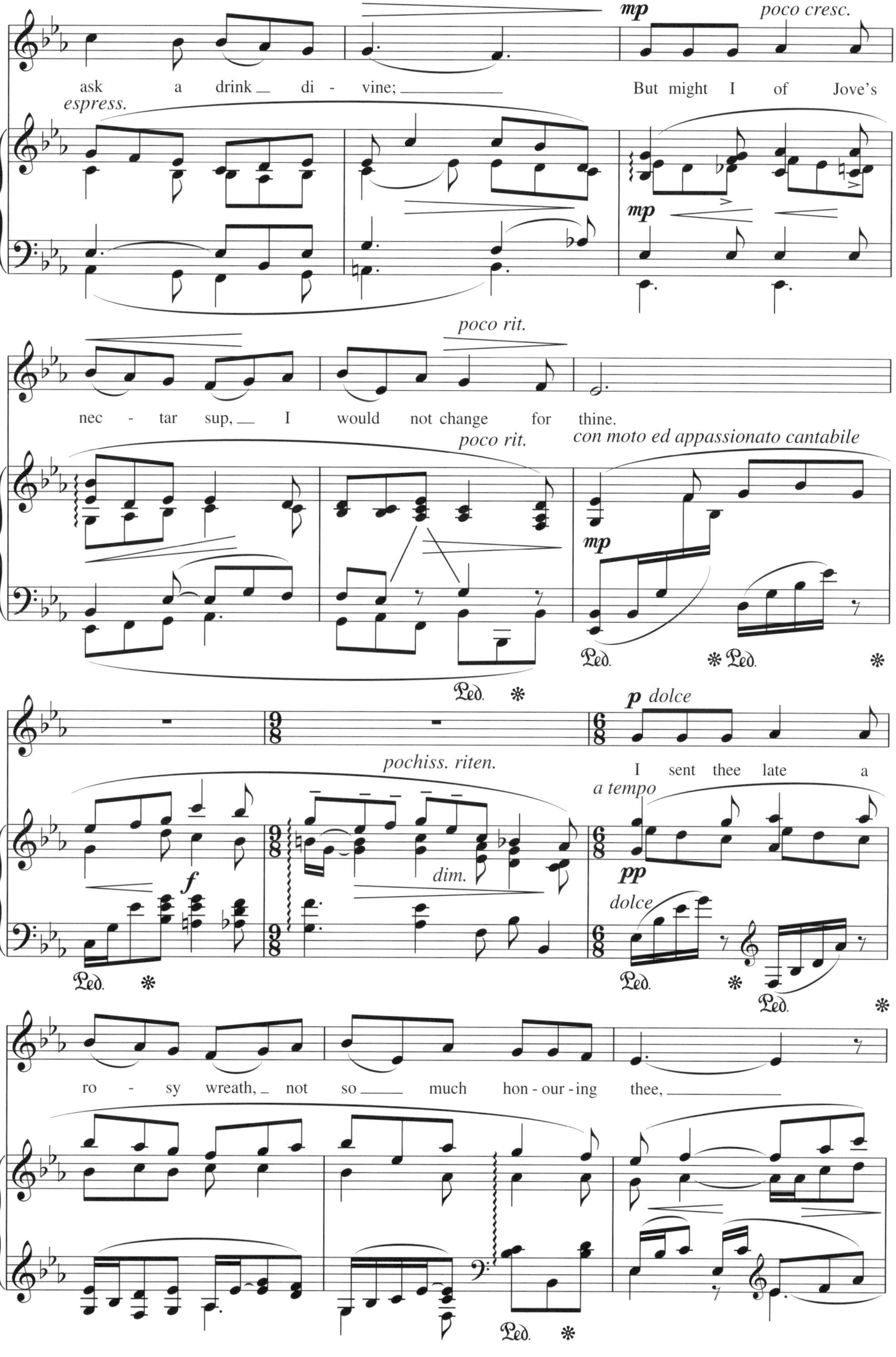
mp
poco cresc.
ask a drink di - vine; But might I of Jove's
espress.
mp
poco rit.
nec - tar sup, I would not change for thine.
poco rit.
con moto ed appassionato cantabile
mp
Ped.
Ped.
p dolce
I sent thee late a
pochiss. riten.
a tempo
f
dim.
pp
dolce
Ped.
Ped.
Ped.
ro - sy wreath, not so much hon - our - ing thee,
Ped.

For Joseph Farrington

THE JOLLY MILLER

from *Old English Popular Songs*
original key

Words Anonymous
from *Love in a Village*, 1762

old English melody
arranged by
Roger Quilter

212

For Theodore Byard

OVER THE MOUNTAINS
from *Old English Popular Songs*
original key: G Major

Words from Thomas Percy's collection of ballads *Reliques*

Air from *Musick's Recreation on the Lyra Viol*, 1652
arranged by Roger Quilter

Allegro con moto (♩ = 144)

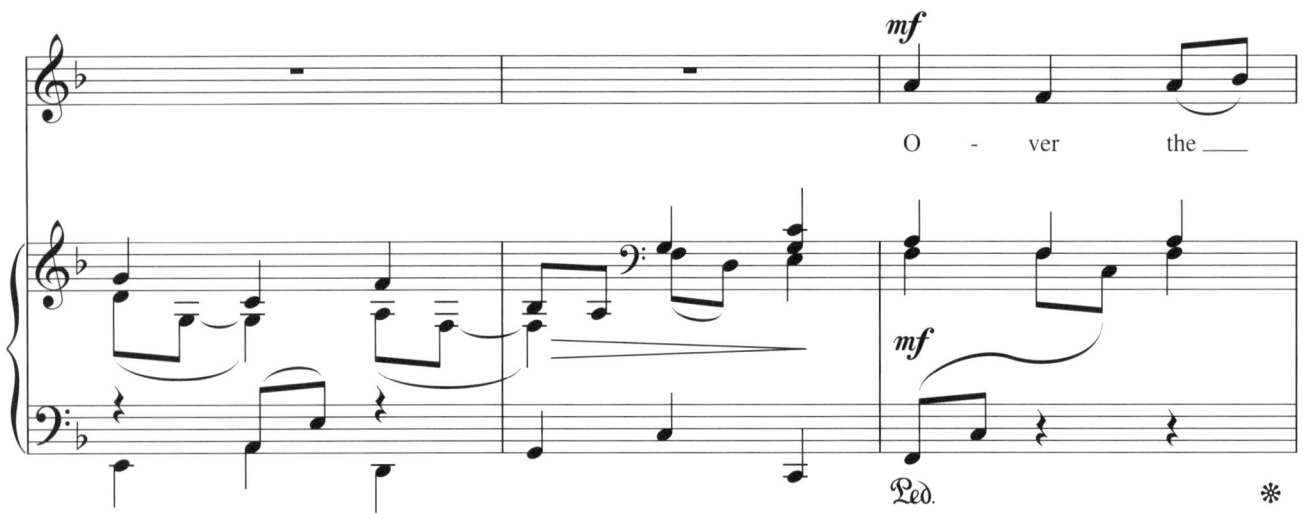

Copyright © 2003 by HAL LEONARD CORPORATION
International Copyright Secured   All Rights Reserved

For Guy Vivian

THREE POOR MARINERS

from *Old English Popular Songs*

original key

Words and Air from Freeman's Songs
in *Deuteromelia*, 1609
arranged by
Roger Quilter

Notes on the Songs

Three Songs of the Sea, Op. 1

The Sea-Bird
Moonlight
By the Sea

Composed 1900. In its original form, the set was *Four Songs of the Sea*. First performed at the Crystal Palace, London, March 11, 1901, by baritone Denham Price and Quilter as pianist. Published by Forsyth Bros. Quilter revised the text (by RQ) and music for a 1911 edition, eliminating the song "I Have a Friend." The songs were dedicated to the composer's mother, Lady Mary Quilter (b. 1840, d. 1927); mother and son were particularly devoted to one another.

Two Songs (1903)

Come Back!
A Secret

"A Secret" was composed in 1898; "Come Back!" probably dates from the same year. Published by Elkin, 1903. Withdrawn by the composer in 1915.

from Three Songs, Op. 3

Quilter designated these as Op. 3, though the songs were apparently not composed as a set.

Love's Philosophy

Composed c1905. Probaby first performed by tenor Gervase Elwes, to whom the song is dedicated, with Quilter as pianist. Published by Boosey and Co., 1905. Published by Schott in German translation, 1924. Elwes (1866-1921) was a celebrated concert singer, and Quilter's favorite. Elwes' voice was not especially large, but was well-suited to recital. He sang with clarity, finesse and sensitivity. This is one of the most recorded of Quilter songs. Recordings include those by John Aler, Arleen Auger, Janet Baker, Gervase Elwes, Elizabeth Harwood, Felicity Lott, John McCormack, Peter Pears, Rosa Ponselle, Joan Sutherland, and others. Quilter recorded the song with baritone Mark Raphael in 1934, and with baritone Frederick Harvey in 1945; both recordings are included on the CD packaged with *Roger Quilter: His Life and Music* by Valerie Langfield, The Boydell Press, 2002.

Now sleeps the crimson petal

Composed 1897, one of Quilter's first songs. Revised c1904. Published by Boosey and Co., 1904. Further later revisions were made for a 1946 edition. This volume presents the 1904 version. Published by Schott in German translation, 1924. Possible first performance April 23, 1904, Bechstein Hall, London, tenor Gervase Elwes, Quilter at the piano. This is the most recorded Quilter song. Recordings include those by Thomas Allen, Ian Bostridge, Gervase Elwes, Kathleen Ferrier, John McCormack, Peter Pears, Paul Robeson, Robert White, and others.

June (1905)

Composed c1905. Published by Boosey and Co., 1905. Probably composed for and first performed by soprano Ada Crossley, to whom the song is dedicated.

from Four Child Songs, Op. 5

A Good Child
The Lampligher
Where Go the Boats?

Composed c1905. Published by Chappell, 1914. The last song of the set, "Foreign Children," was omitted from the current compilation due to its quite outdated British imperialist viewpoint. Quilter revised two of the songs, "A Good Child" and "Where Go the Boats?," for a 1945 Chappell edition. This volume presents the 1914 versions. The set was dedicated to Quilter's second oldest sister, Norah Blanche Quilter Vivian, mother to two young children at the time of composition.

Three Shakespeare Songs, Op. 6 (First Set)

Come away, death
O mistress mine
Blow, blow, thou winter wind

Composed 1905. Published as a set by Boosey and Co., 1905. Published by Schott in German translation, 1920s. The songs are linked by key, but are a carefully planned grouping rather than a song cycle. The set was dedicated to Quilter's close friend Walter Creighton (1878-1958), a singer in his youth and the artist who premiered Ralph Vaughan Williams' *Songs of Travel*. Quilter made arrangements of the songs for voice and piano trio, voice and piano quartet, and voice and orchestra. The songs have sometimes been used in productions of Shakespeare plays. The set and individual songs have been often recorded. An arrangement for voice and piano quartet of "Come away, death" was recorded by Quilter (piano) and baritone Mark Raphael in 1934, released on the CD packaged with *Roger Quilter: His Life and Music* by Valerie Langfield, The Boydell Press, 2002. Quilter also accompanies the other two songs from the set on the same CD. Other highlight recordings: "Come away, death" by Ian Bostridge; "O mistress mine" by Peter Pears and Benjamin Britten, Paul Robeson; "Blow, blow, thou winter wind" by Marian Anderson, Jan Peerce.

To Julia, Op. 8

Prelude
The Bracelet
The Maiden Blush
To Daisies
The Night Piece
Julia's Hair
Interlude
Cherry Ripe

Composed 1905 for tenor Gervase Elwes (see "Love's Philosophy"), who premiered the piece with Quilter on October 31, 1905, Aeolian Hall, London. Published by Boosey and Co., 1906. This is Quilter's only proper song cycle. The poems were chosen from the large Robert Herrick collection *Hesperides*, published in 1648. Quilter's 1936 light opera *Julia* probably bore no relation to the song cycle, except the composer's partiality to the name. Quilter later made an arrangement of the cycle for voice and piano quintet, and also one for voice and string quartet. The composer directed a 1923 recording of the latter arrangement, included on the CD packaged with Valerie Langfield's *Roger Quilter: His Life and Music*, The Boydell Press, 2002. Quilter also made violin and piano transcriptions of "To Daisies" (unpublished), "Julia's Hair" (published by Boosey and Co., 1919), and "Love Song to Julia" ("Cherry Ripe") (published by Boosey and Co., 1919). "Julia's Hair" was also transcribed for cello and piano (published by Boosey and Co., 1919).

Seven Elizabethan Lyrics, Op. 12

Weep you no more
My Life's Delight
Damask Roses
The Faithless Shepherdess
Brown is my love
By a Fountainside
Fair House of Joy

Composed 1907. First performance most likely by tenor Gervase Elwes (see "Love's Philosophy") and Quilter, November 17, 1908, Bechstein Hall, London. Published as a set by Boosey and Co., 1908. Quilter rejected two songs originally composed for the set and wrote two new songs before the premiere. The texts for these songs had been variously published in collections. The set was dedicated to the memory of Gervase Elwes' mother, Alice Cary-Elwes, who died in 1907. The set and its individual songs have been recorded by several artists; "Weep you no more" and "Fair House of Joy" are the most often recorded, the first by Elly Ameling and others, the latter by Kathleen Ferrier and others. Quilter arranged "Weep you no more" as a vocal duet in 1938. The composer made various arrangements of some songs of the set for voice and orchestra. "Weep you no more" was also arranged by the composer for women's chorus.

Four Songs, Op. 14

Autumn Evening
April
A Last Year's Rose
Song of the Blackbird

Composed 1909-1910. Published by Boosey and Co., 1910. In *Roger Quilter: His Life and Music*, author Valerie Langfield writes, based on viewing the composer's autobiographical notes, "…the opening notes of the last song were taken from those of a real blackbird that Quilter had heard. Just after finishing the manuscripts of 'Autumn Evening' and 'Song of the Blackbird,' he left them in a taxi. They were never found, and he 'had to think them all over again.'" "Song of the Blackbird" was recorded by Quilter and baritone Mark Raphael, included in the CD packaged with Langfield's book.

Six Songs, Op. 18

Three Songs for Baritone or Tenor:
To Wine and Beauty
Where be you going?
The Jocund Dance

The Spring is at the door

Two September Songs:
Through the sunny garden
The Valley and the Hill

Though grouped by the composer under the same opus number, these six songs are really of three distinctions. The first three are more a true set, composed in 1913. The fourth song, composed in 1914, is a separate entity; the last two songs, composed in 1916, are another set. The first four songs were published individually by Elkin, 1914; the first three were subsequently released as *Three Songs for Baritone or Tenor* in 1920. (The very title reveals something significant about the composer's liberal view about transposition of his songs.) *Two September Songs* were published as a set by Elkin, 1916. The composer's alternate title for "To Wine and Beauty," crossed out in the manuscript, was "Bacchus Song." It is dedicated to Theodore Byard, an actor friend. "The Jocund Dance" was dedicated to friend and composer Frederic Austin. Though there is no apparent record of performance, the final two songs of the opus were probably premiered by Muriel Foster, a singer to whom they were dedicated. "Where be you going?" was recorded by Quilter and baritone Mark Raphael, included in the CD packaged with *Roger Quilter: His Life and Music*, by Valerie Langfield, The Boydell Press, 2002.

Three Songs of William Blake, Op. 20

Dream Valley
The Wild Flower's Song
Daybreak

The first was composed in 1916, the remaining songs in 1917. First performed by Muriel Foster and Quilter, December 14, 1917, Wigmore Hall, London. Published by Winthrop Rogers, 1917.

Three Pastoral Songs, Op. 22

I will go with my father a-ploughing
Cherry Valley
I wish and I wish

Composed 1920. The set was originally scored for piano trio. Elkin published it in 1921 with and without string parts. Though the premiere performance is unknown, the African-American baritone Roland Hayes, a friend of Quilter's whom the composer artistically encouraged, performed two of the songs in Paris in 1924 with the composer at the piano. "Cherry Valley" with string parts was recorded by Quilter and baritone Mark Raphael, included in the CD packaged with Valerie Langfield's *Roger Quilter: His Life and Music*, The Boydell Press, 2002.

Five Shakespeare Songs, Op. 23 (Second Set)

Fear no more the heat o' the sun
Under the greenwood tree
It was a lover and his lass
Take, O take those lips away
Hey, ho, the wind and the rain

Three of the songs were composed in 1919. "Fear no more" was composed in 1921. "It was a lover and his lass" was originally composed as a duet in 1919; the solo version was composed in 1921. Unlike the Shakespeare songs of Op. 6, which are conceptually linked, this opus is simply a collection of songs. The first song of the set was dedicated to the memory of Robin Hollway, Quilter's friend from Oxford who died in suicide in 1921. Three of the songs were dedicated to Quilter's close friend Walter Creighton, a singer in his youth and the artist who premiered Ralph Vaughan Williams' *Songs of Travel*. The songs have been often recorded. Among others, Peter Pears recorded "Fear no more;" Janet Baker was among the artists who recorded "It was a lover and his lass." The first, third and fourth songs were recorded by Quilter and baritone Mark Raphael, recordings included on the CD packaged with *Roger Quilter: His Life and Music*, by Valerie Langfield, The Boydell Press, 2002.

Two Songs, Op. 26

In the highlands
Over the land is April

Composed 1922. Published by Elkin, 1922. "Over the land is April" was recorded by Quilter and baritone Mark Raphael, included on the CD packaged with *Roger Quilter: His Life and Music*, by Valerie Langfield, The Boydell Press, 2002.

Old English Popular Songs

Barbara Allen
Drink to Me Only with Thine Eyes
The Jolly Miller
Over the Mountains
Three Poor Mariners

Composed c1917-1921. Published individually by Winthrop Rogers, 1921. Quilter made arrangements for piano trio of "Drink to Me Only" and "Three Poor Mariners," calling the set *Two Old English Tunes* (published by Winthrop Rogers, 1917). In the 1940s Quilter included the five songs first known as *Old English Popular Songs* in *The Arnold Book of Old Songs*, dedicated to Arnold Vivian, the composer's favorite nephew who was killed in World War II. Though individual sheets had been previously released, the assembled collection was first published by Boosey & Hawkes, 1950.

Sources Consulted:

Stephen Banfield, *Sensibility and English Song* (Cambridge University Press, 1985).

Percy Grainger, *The Farthest North of Humanness: Letters of Percy Grainger 1901-1914,* ed. Kay Dreyfus (Melbourne: MMB Music, Inc., 1985).

Percy Grainger, *The All-Round Man: Selected Letters of Percy Grainger 1914-1961,* ed. Malcom Gilles and David Pear (Oxford University Press, 1994).

Trevor Hold: *The Walled-In Garden: A Study of the Songs of Roger Quilter* (London: Thames, 1996).

Salan Keiler, *Marian Anderson: A Singer's Journey* (New York: Simon & Schuster, 2000).

Valerie Langfield, *Roger Quilter: His Life and Music* (Woodbridge, Suffolk: The Boydell Pres, 2002).

The New Grove Dictionary of Music and Musicians, ed. S. Sadie and J. Tyrrell (London: Macmillan, 2001).

Michael Pilkington, *English Solo Song Guides to the Repertoire of Gurney, Ireland, Quilter, Warlock* (London: Duckworth, 1989).

Also in THE VOCAL LIBRARY

POPULAR BALLADS FOR CLASSICAL SINGERS
Concert Arrangements by Richard Walters
00740138 High Voice
00740139 Low Voice

Wonderfully complex, sophisticated and stylish art music arrangements of classic songs by Richard Rodgers, Cole Porter and George Gershwin, designed for a classical singer and pianist. As one performer put it, "The arrangements are so rich they become art songs on their own." **Rodgers songs:** The Sweetest Sounds • I Have Dreamed • You're Nearer. **Porter songs:** I Am in Love • I Concentrate on You • I Hate You Darling. **Gershwin songs:** They Can't Take That Away from Me • A Foggy Day/Love Walked In • Nice Work If You Can Get It • Love Is Here to Stay.

THE CHRISTMAS COLLECTION
Edited by Richard Walters
00740153 High Voice
00740154 Low Voice

A large resource of over 50 songs for holiday services and events, designed for a lifetime of use. Material includes art songs, classic popular songs, and arrangements for solo voice and piano. A few bonus duets are included, and selected songs have solo instrumental obbligatos.

CONTENTS: *Art Songs/Traditional Songs*—A Christmas Carol (Dello Joio) • The Birthday of a King (Neidlinger) • Bright Star (Dello Joio) • Epiphanias (Wolf) • Ermuntre Dich (Bach) • Gesù Bambino (Yon) • Holy Infant's Lullaby • I Stand Here at the Cradleside (duet) (Karg-Elert) • I Wonder as I Wander (Niles) • Jesus of Nazareth (Gounod) • Noël des enfants qui n'ont plus de masions (Debussy) • Nun wandre Maria (Wolf) • O Holy Night (Adam) • O Jesulein süss (Bach) • Schlafendes Jesuskind (Wolf) • A Slumber Song of the Madonna (Head) • The Virgin's Slumber Song (Reger) • *Weihnachtslieder* (Cornelius) • What Songs Were Sung (Niles). ***Carol Arrangements, most arr. by Richard Walters***—Angels We Have Heard on High (Les anges dans nos campagnes) (duet) • Bring a Torch, Jeannette, Isabella (Un flambeau, Jeanette, Isabelle) (with violin) • Caroling, Caroling • Deck the Hall (with flute) • The First Noel • Go, Tell It on the Mountain • The Holly and the Ivy (duet, with flute) • I Saw Three Ships • In the Bleak Midwinter • It Came Upon the Midnight Clear • Jesus, Jesus, Rest Your Head • Lo, How a Rose E'er Blooming (with violin) • O Hearken Ye • Once in Royal David's City • Silent Night • Some Children See Him • The Star Carol • This Is Christmas • Wexford Carol. ***Classic Popular Christmas Songs***—The Christmas Song (arr. Walters) • The Christmas Waltz • Do You Hear What I Hear • I Heard the Bells on Christmas Day • I'll Be Home for Christmas • The Most Wonderful Time of the Year • Silver Bells • White Christmas (arr. Walters).

Also in THE VOCAL LIBRARY

THE SACRED COLLECTION
Edited by Richard Walters
00740155 High Voice
00740156 Low Voice

A huge collection of 70 sacred songs for classical singers, spanning an enormous range of literature, including art songs, traditional songs, classic Burleigh spiritual arrangements (experts on African-American spirituals contend they are for singers of all ethnic heritages), and distinctive concert arrangements of hymns and folksongs by Richard Walters. There are four duets included. This collection will be as useful in the voice studio as in every working singer's repertoire and every church music library.

CONTENTS: *Sacred Art Songs/Traditional Sacred Songs*—Agnus Dei (Bizet) • Ave Maria (Franck) • Ave Maria (Schubert) • Ave Maria (Bach/Gounod) • Be Near Me Still (Hiller) • Biblical Songs (Dvořák) *complete set* (Clouds and Darkness • Lord, Thou Art My Refuge • Hear My Prayer • God Is My Shepherd • I Will Sing New Songs • Hear My Prayer, O Lord • By the Waters of Babylon • Turn Thee to Me • I Will Lift Up Mine Eyes • Sing Ye a Joyful Song • Bist du bei mir (Stölzel, previously attributed to Bach) • Crucifixus (Faure) • Dank sei Dir, Herr (Ochs, previously attributed to Handel) • Entreat Me Not to Leave Thee (Gounod) • Evening Hymn (Purcell) • Evening Prayer from *Hansel and Gretel* (duet) (Humperdinck) • He That Keepeth Israel (Schlösser) • The Holy City (Weatherly and Adams) • Jesu, Joy of Man's Desiring (Bach) • O Divine Redeemer (Gounod) • The Palms (Fauré) • Panis Angelicus (Franck) • There Is a Green Hill Far Away (Gounod). **Spirituals, Arr. by Harry T. Burleigh**—Balm in Gilead • By an' By • Couldn't Hear Nobody Pray • Deep River • Didn't My Lord Deliver Daniel • Don't You Weep When I'm Gone • Go Down, Moses • Go, Tell It on the Mountain • The Gospel Train • He's Just the Same Today • I Don't Feel No-Ways Tired • I Stood on the River of Jordan • I Want to Be Ready • Let Us Cheer the Weary Traveler • Little David, Play on Your Harp • My Lord, What a Mornin' • My Way's Cloudy • Nodoby Knows the Trouble I've Seen • O Rocks, Don't Fall on Me • Oh, Didn't It Rain • Sinner, Please Don't Let This Harvest Pass • Sometimes I Feel Like a Motherless Child • Steal Away • Swing Low, Sweet Chariot • 'Tis Me, O Lord • Wade in the Water • Weepin' Mary • You May Bury Me in the East. **Concert Arrangements of Hymns & Sacred Folksongs, Arr. by Richard Walters**—Ah, Holy Jesus • All Creatures of Our God and King (duet) • Be Thou My Vision • Come, Thou Fount of Every Blessing • How Can I Keep from Singing (duet) • How Firm a Foundation • Just a Closer Walk with Thee • Let Us Break Bread Together • Now Thank We All Our God • O for a Thousand Tongues to Sing • Praise to the Lord, the Almighty • This Is My Father's World • We Are Climbing Jacob's Ladder (duet) • Wondrous Love (duet).

Also in THE VOCAL LIBRARY

FRANZ SCHUBERT: 100 SONGS
Edited by Steven Stolen & Richard Walters
00740027 High Voice
00740028 Low Voice

A major new edition, newly researched, with new music engravings, historical notes on each song, a poet index and line by line translations for study. Unlike other Schubert editions, the complete cycles *Die Winterreise* and *Die schöne Müllerin* are deliberately not included, since in their entirety they are not useful to most singers. (*Schwanengesang* is included in its entirety, however.) This leaves a great deal of room for a rich selection of individual songs. In the introductory notes for each song you will find information about the song's composition, its biographical context in Schubert's life, early performances, and comments about poets.

CONTENTS: Abendstern • Abschied • Am Grabe Anselmos • Am See (Bruchmann) • Am See (Mayrhofer) • An den Mond (Goethe) • An den Mond (Hölty) • An den Tod • An die Entfernte • An die Geliebte • An die Laute • An die Leier • An die Musik • An die Nachtigall • An die Sonne • An Schwager Kronos • An Silvia • Auf dem Strom *(high voice only)* • Auf dem Wasser zu singen • Auf der Bruck • Das Abendrot *(low voice only)* • Dass sie hier gewesen! • Der Alpenjäger • Der Hirt auf dem Felsen *(high voice only)* • Der Jüngling an der Quelle • Der König in Thule • Der Musensohn • Der Neugierige • Der Tod und das Mädchen • Der Wanderer • Der Zwerg • Die Allmacht • Die böse Farbe • Die Forelle • Die junge Nonne • Die liebe Farbe • Die Liebe hat gelogen • Die Männer sind méchant! • Die Unterscheidung • Du bist die Ruh • Du liebst mich nicht • Ellens Gesang I (Raste Krieger) • Ellens Gesang II (Jäger, ruhe von der Jagd!) • Ellens Gesang III (Ave Maria!) • Erlafsee • Erlkönig • Erster Verlust • Frühlingsglaube • Ganymed • Geheimes • Grenzen der Menschheit • Gretchen am Spinnrade • Gruppe aus dem Tartarus • Heidenröslein • Heliopolis I • Heliopolis II • Herbst • Hoffnung • Im Abendrot • Im Frühling • Im Haine • Im Walde • Jägers Abendlied • Klaglied • Lachen und Weinen • Liebe schwärmt auf allen Wegen • Lied der Mignon (Heiß mich nicht reden) • Lied der Mignon (So lasst mich scheinen) • Lied der Mignon (Nur wer die Sehnsucht kennt) • Litanei • Meeres Stille • Memnon • Mignons Gesang (Kennst du das Land?) • Nacht und Träume • Nachtstück • Nachtviolen • Rastlose Liebe • Romanze *(low voice only)* • Schäfers Klagelied) • *Schwanengesang:* Liebesbotschaft • Kriegers Ahnung • Frühlingssehnsucht • Ständchen (Rellstab) • Aufenthalt • In der Ferne • Abschied (Rellstab) • Der Atlas • Ihr Bild • Das Fischermädchen • Die Stadt • Am Meer • Der Doppelgänger • Die Taubenpost • Sehnsucht • Sei mir gegrüßt • Seligkeit • Ständchen (Shakespeare) • Suleika I • Verklärung • Wandrers Nachtlied I • Wandrers Nachtlied II • Wohin?

Prices, contents and availability subject to change without notice.

Visit Hal Leonard online at **www.halleonard.com**